BIRTHMARK

BIRTHMARK

Lorraine Dusky

M. Evans and Company, Inc.   New York

The names of some of the individuals in this book have been changed to protect their privacy; in addition, some locations have been purposely obscured, and the names of certain places changed.

Library of Congress Cataloging in Publication Data
Dusky, Lorraine.
  Birthmark.

  1. Dusky, Lorraine.   2. Mothers—United States—
Biography.   3. Adoption—United   States.   I. Title.
HQ759.D865   301.42′7   79-16273
ISBN 0-87131-299-9

M. Evans and Company, Inc.
216 East 49 Street
New York, New York 10017

Design by Ginger Giles

Manufactured in the United States of America

9 8 7 6 5 4 3 2 1

To my daughter

Acknowledgments

I first began writing this book thirteen years ago when I started typing out notes to my child. Vignettes followed, and were read and criticized by the person I call Brian. These jottings were filed away for years; I was unaware that they would come together as a book. The idea was planted by a friend and editor, Robert Shnayerson, when he told me that his magazine was not right for the piece I had submitted. "Why don't you turn it into a book?" he asked. Indeed, why not? Within days, I had begun. Over the five years since then, he has read, offered editorial help, and beyond that, given advice and support whenever they were needed.

The person who was instrumental in bringing this work to its present form is Peter Dee, the playwright. We met when he was the night watchman and desk clerk at the Sea Cliff Inn on Nantucket and I was the hostess in the dining room. Peter and I read each other's poetry that summer, and when he came upon one poem of mine about a missing daughter, he had the innocence and integrity to suggest that I only write on topics about which I knew something. I said nothing at the time, but when I began my book, Peter was there to read, send me home to rewrite, and read again. And again. I do not know what I would have done without him.

Beyond that, I feel that I have been blessed with an abundance of friends who freely gave me their time, support, and the confidence to continue when it seemed that I would never get the words down on paper the *right* way. In particular, I want to thank John Baldwin for his unquestioning belief in this project the day after we met, and especially for a late night long-distance phone call when a letter conveyed my discouragement; Rhoda Weyr for being so much more than simply a good agent—from the first phone call on; Barbara King, Diana Davenport, Rita Watson, Angela Miller, and Gay Hemingway and John Duffy for their unique contributions and for being the kind of friends who make you feel that you need not look further for a special affinity; William Iversen, Barry Stainbach, and Kathryn Livingston for their time and suggestions; Linda Cabasin for her patience and assistance; Herb Katz, my publisher, for signing the book so quickly; and my mother for standing behind me. To all of the above, and to many chance acquaintances who were encouraging, and to the people who have become characters in this story, I offer my heartfelt gratitude and thanks. Somehow this does not seem enough.

I have read and enjoyed the plays of Aeschylus and Sophocles. A few lines from Aeschylus's *Prometheus Bound, The Libation Bearers,* and *Agamemnon* and Sophocles's *Oedipus at Colonus* appear in the book.

1

A Case of Identity

To meet me, you wouldn't think anything was wrong. Blonde lady in her thirties. Laughs a lot. Writes for a living. You would assume that due to choice and circumstance, I had not taken time out to have a child, which as you know gets in the way of a career. I smile and make small talk. Then it's my turn to ask a question.

Is that your daughter?

I have a daughter too. But I never saw her. One minute she was in me, and the next minute she was gone. I gave her away. She was adopted, I mean. Do you understand? I'm one of those *biological mothers*. I could tell you what happened so that it would sound perfectly reasonable that I gave her away—what else could a poor girl have done back in 1966? But I know that for whatever reasons, no matter that any psychiatrist would try to convince me that I did right by her and myself, I gave her away to an uncertain future with people who might turn out to be all right. The point is, I don't know that. I simply removed her from my life so that I could go on living the life I'd always dreamed about. That year would be skimmed over when I was making out résumés and filling out forms for *Who's Who of American Women.* Of course I knew I would always remember her, but I didn't think it would be most of the time. I thought I could outsmart my gender by doing all the career things the right way, the way men did them. I made the choice between children and a career a long time ago. Or so I thought. What I succeeded in doing was splitting myself into a sort of yin and yang within one frame. Look at me: That daughter I do not have has given birth to a career. I write about her, or adoption, or opening those closed records that keep us apart forever, those records with my name and her new name on them. I even talk about it on TV.

Sometimes the reruns are on and I find out the next morning when a viewer calls, wanting to know how to go about finding his or her mother. But in the meantime, I'll do as a surrogate mother. They want to know is it OK to look for the real mother? She won't be mad, will she? She won't reject me, will she?

Not if she's anything like me.

You see, I am always looking for my daughter: girl, weighing four pounds four ounces at birth, April 5, 1966, in upstate New York. Baptized: Mary. Her birth is the single most important event of my life; since that day, her existence has shaped who I am. I live in the hope that someday I might be able to telephone her on her birthday and send her flowers or a ticket to someplace she would like to go. I would like to ask her how things turned out and if her parents are nice to her and if they love her.

I know, I know, I gave her away, I can hear you

thinking; I knew what I was doing and so why am I making a fuss now?

A signature cannot abrogate my feelings.

As things stand now, the yearning and searching will go on until I find her.

The adoptees I've talked to say they need to know whence they came; I need to know where I am going. And until that day comes, I will go on looking for my daughter at shopping centers, in the little girl who lives upstairs, in the child I saw three summers ago at Paradise Island, in pictures in magazines. Every time I hear that so-and-so has an adopted daughter, I have to stop and tell myself that it couldn't be she. Yet I find myself asking How old is she? as if the words had been programmed into me without my consent, and I am helpless to stop them. And if the age is the same as hers, I will find some way to pin down the specific birthdate. The statistics tell me that she is one of 72,800 children adopted by nonrelatives in 1967, the year the adoption would have been final, which makes my chances of finding her this way a statistical absurdity. What else is there to do?

I have to admit I have considered hiring a burglar to break into the adoption agency and steal our file.

We are on Long Island Sound on the Connecticut shore, and her three kids are outside flying kites, Japanese butterflies and such, strung out far over the water, dots on the landscape. I've come to dinner with a friend of her husband. The barrier between this woman and me is suffocating. We have only exchanged pleasantries, but in a way I can't quite pin down, she is angry with me, as if somehow my existence offends her. I am not sure there is anything I can do to change that. The strikes are against me because I work; because I do not have children. It is not the words she is using, it is how she is saying them—with an arch of a brow, a pursing of the lips, an underlying edge in the voice.

Maybe if I said, yes, my career is jiggling along just fine, but I still worry about paying the rent, would that cut through the ice? Maybe she feels that I am critical of her because her occupation is wife/mother, but that's the last thing on my mind. I understand exactly why being a homemaker is a fine way to make a life. All right, it's true that among my close friends, except for a woman I've known since kindergarten, there are none who are full-time mothers. But then neither do I know a lot of cabdrivers or nurses, and I bet she doesn't either. Life's not like that. Maybe she is nervous because her husband has been taking my picture with his Polaroid because this is the day I've signed a contract for my first book, and he's making a fuss, and we used to go together, but that was a few years ago. Maybe she pities me, I wouldn't be surprised. A barren career woman, without the proper accouterments of a respectable life: husband, house, babies. It never seemed to me I had that choice. I grew up knowing that if a woman wanted to have a career the way men have careers, something had to go, and that was a family. Now a lot has changed; women have careers, and men have families, more or less. But I've made my bed and now I must lie in it.

I want to go outside and fly kites. I do not play with children as often as I would like. They are hard to come by in my life, and I don't care whether this woman thinks I'm strange or not.

"When will Jennifer be eleven?" I ask, half as a question, half to fill the silent air.

"In a few weeks. April fifteenth." Ten days after my daughter's birthday. Now what?

"Do you mind—I think I'll go outside and fly kites. I don't get out of the city often enough." And I want to talk to your daughter, to find out what it is like to be ten going on eleven.

With three kids and three kites and the wind chancy and one budding stepfather and me, there is a lot of commotion. Jennifer's younger sister does perfect cartwheels, and the youngest needs my help with his kite, threatening to go down in a bay of mud now that the tide's out. Jennifer and I never get past the vagaries of kite flying. I can't ask what she thinks of boys and does she have a special boyfriend and what are her favorite subjects in school and does she like to read and can she swim and does she know how to twirl a baton? These are the questions I want to put to my own ten-year-old. With Jennifer, I am tongue-tied and suddenly quite shy.

Ten. That was the year I decided to be a writer. On the Day of the Banana. For a geography assignment, we had to personify a banana growing up in South America, and bring that banana all the way to our homes in Michigan. I wrote my paper the night before it was due. When the nun returned them a few days later, she read "one special one" to the class. She didn't say whose it was until she finished, and while she was reading and everybody was listening, I decided right then and there that I would be a writer. I would live in a garret, preferably in Paris, and I would sit around cafés drinking wine with smart friends, artists and writers and maybe people from the theater, when I wasn't penning poetry and prose. There certainly wasn't a baby by my side.

And then Sister Felicia said I had written the story,

and everybody turned around to look at me, and I had never felt so proud. That day still ranks as one of my all-time highs. You only get a couple no matter how long you live.

Being a writer made sense out of the fact that I didn't play with the kids much or help my mother fix dinner, both of which annoyed her. I went to the library almost every day after school or holed up in my room with books. Being a writer made sense out of the fact that I always had a few hiding places no one else knew about, where I could sit and think for an hour or more.

After that day, my life was more or less arranged. You make one strong choice, and all the others fall into place. A few years later, it occurred to me that I couldn't get tied down with a man and children. None of my aunts, none of the ladies of Dearborn, none of the grown-up female persons I knew did anything but take care of children full time. Oh, there was one aunt who went to New York, but I saw her only two weeks every other year when she came to visit. She smoked and she drank and she bet at the racetrack. She certainly seemed like the most interesting person I knew who was female.

One more thing—I didn't grow up pretty, so I wasn't distracted by boys and romance. Had this huge nose, you see, that people used to stare at. I'm not kidding, it really was that big. It was long and thin and pointed and had a spectacular bump. I had it fixed after the baby was born. Upholding my individuality for the sake of an intellectual principle was much too troublesome.

I have succeeded at what I set out to do: I write, I have quick and brainy friends, and I have lived in a garret, although it turned out to be in Manhattan. Yet something is drastically wrong. There is a cross fire of confusion deep within me. Never mind that some women tell me I am fortunate always to have known what I wanted to do, to be able to take care of myself, to be able to pack my bags when whim and pocketbook are so inclined, to not be waking up at thirty-five and deciding that the husband and children are not enough. I wake up at thirty-six and wonder about the daughter who got away. She is everywhere.

Another couple arrives and there is a lot of commotion and music all evening, and Jennifer's mother and I avoid having a real conversation the rest of the night. Later, I hear she thinks I am distant, unfriendly, condescending. Later still, she and I somehow end up having lunch and I end up telling her the whole story and we both are sad and then things relax.

I read in a book by Margaret Drabble that the world is divided into two groups: those who have children and those who don't. I am not so sure it makes that much difference to the men, but for the women, it surely does. Me? Well, I can flit back and forth into either group. I fit in both, I fit in neither. Sort of. The women who don't have children sometimes forget that I ever did, and the women who do, never forget.

There are lots of times I've told a woman that I too have a child, somewhere out there, just to get through to her; then somebody confides that she was pregnant before she was wed, and that's how her life was arranged.

My life took a different turn. I fell in love with a man already married; a child was born. I gave her up for adoption. But I did not forget: She pervades my being.

This is our story: two women marked by birth.

2

The Matter of Conception

Brian was a reporter on the newspaper where I worked. Older. Someone who would actually help me with my writing. A mentor, you could say. Safely married, he wouldn't ask me to give it all up and bear his children. Not like the boys I knew in college. Not like the one I almost married before I left Michigan. At the time, I would have said *escaped*.

I was twenty-two, less than a year out of college, and was leaving a job writing up Alençon lace and peau de soie weddings, which a few of us called Sweaty Brides, for a small-town newspaper in Saginaw, Michigan. The new job, offered by a friend of a friend of mine, was in upstate New York (at least the same state as Manhattan) on a bigger paper in a bigger city, and it was definitely not covering *kinder, kuche, und kirche*. Not that I had ever wanted to, but I had no choice when I left college. No matter that my credentials were better than most men my age, no matter that I said I wanted to work cityside, I simply was not offered a position out of the women's department. But in the new job, I would get to work side by side with the guys, and I would be the only woman in a decade to do so. When the paper offered to fly me to town for a tryout, I told my parents I was only going for the ride. I would not know a soul there. I began packing as soon as I was offered the job.

From the beginning I knew Brian was married, right from the first day. Since it was a morning paper, cityside reporters worked afternoons and evenings, and lunch was really dinner, falling somewhere between six and eight, depending on whether you were writing for the first edition deadline of 8:45 P.M. The few other women on the paper were usually long gone by the time dinner came, and although the men had been friendly enough that afternoon when I was assigned a desk in the city room, no one asked me to go over to the usual hangout and share a beer and a steak sandwich. Even if I had known about the place, I would have been much too shy to walk in alone. Because I was a woman, and because the paper had imported me from the Midwest, I think they regarded me with more curiosity than friendship. The hotshot from Michigan had to prove her stuff before she was welcomed into the club.

Owen, the city editor, took me under his wing and decided to take me over to Billy's and introduce me around, before he went home for the night. He asked his best friend to come along. But when we got to the street and passed Owen's Volks on the way, he changed his mind and said he thought he might just go on home, since he was through for the night, and besides, Brian would take care of me, right?

Now what?

I felt quite stupid, being forced on Brian this way. He was The Political Columnist. Tall, sandy-haired, and good-looking. I was no beauty who could assume my looks would carry me through dinner. Ever since I had been called "Big Nose" by some boys from school when I was twelve, I knew I couldn't get by simply by being female. I was always an intelligent person who happened to be female. There were lots of times I longed to be a sex object, plain and simple. I know this sounds as if I've got it all wrong.

Brian later told me he thought our first meeting would be one of those tedious hours when he would ask what I took in college and I would respond, and then he would try to think up the next question.

It turned out that he ended up reciting Andrew Marvell's poetry. We both knew we had come upon something good. It was so good, in fact, that the waitress, who knew that the newspaper crowd always got separate checks, asked Brian "One check?" which embarrassed us both. Naturally, I paid for my own linguine and red wine.

But on the walk back to the paper, in the damp, drizzly snow of that February night, I kept brushing up against him. Or at least that is what he told me later, after we were lovers. I am sure he is right. I flourish under a man's affection and tutelage, and I must have been encouraging Brian. I guess it began with Daddy, who taught me to say big words before I was a year old. Now I was a grown woman, that's all.

The next night Brian appeared in front of my desk, already in his trench coat and Irish wool hat, his hands jammed into his pockets. "Going to dinner?"

"YES."

An ice maiden I'll never be.

A month later, Brian and I were in bed. I was feeling uneasy because he was a married man, and I didn't approve of that. I'm not sure I really approved of me in bed with anyone. I had only recently divested myself of my virginity, after the marriage plans with the boy back home fizzled. And you do not obliterate years of listening to the nuns tell you that *it* is a mortal sin, you will go straight to hell for this, without some conscience pangs, no matter how much you intellectualize. The nuns told us that if you held hands with a boy and continued to do so when you felt *the stirrings of passion,* you were doing the devil's work. If hell was this easy to come by, what parlous times lay ahead? When I decided to go all the way, I also decided that I had better become an agnostic.

I guess my guilt was big enough for both of us, because Brian was impotent that night. Maybe he was nervous too, for he wasn't your everyday philanderer. We almost didn't get anywhere the first night. He put on his hat to go and kissed me good-bye at the door, and then came back in to stay awhile.

He was very married, really, with a big house in the suburbs and three young kids, all under ten, and an attractive wife and a two-door Chevy, so the kids wouldn't fall out of the back. He was also a good reporter and writer and cared a great deal about his work. His wife didn't like the long hours he put in for what seemed to her to be low pay, but a reporter has got to be dedicated if he's any good at all, and she resented that too. I could smell trouble right there, but Brian didn't carp on that because he didn't want to give me the wrong idea. In fact, after that first night, when we were having dinner together as usual, he put that right up front.

"Listen, I don't want you to think I'm looking for a way out of my marriage. You have to understand I can't offer you anything. And besides, you're young, you're single . . . you should be . . . you know, out dating other men."

"But *you* have to understand. I *do.* I don't want you to

do anything crazy. That's the last thing I'd want." Good lord, what is he talking about? I don't want to settle down with him. After this place, say a year or two, I want to go to a big-city daily, New York, Chicago, Boston. I want to be the best feature writer in the business. I am not offering marriage.

"That takes a weight off my shoulders. If that's enough, we can go on."

"I'd like that. I don't want to hurt anybody. Is that what you want? It's what I want. It's all I want." How in charge I sounded. We walked up the three flights rather than take the elevator to the city room, and he kissed me in the stairwell, gently and furtively. I was amazed he was taking a chance like that. I didn't want to be caught either.

The day was the Ides of March. The omens were most certainly there, and I most decidedly chose to disregard them.

For a few months, I made an attempt at dating other men, but there weren't many around. True, there were two unmarried men on the newspaper. One was engaged to someone out of town, and the other one got nasty when he drank, which was quite often. It seemed that all the men I met on assignments were married; in this company town of manicured lawns, I stood out like crabgrass. Doing the things that the magazines tell you are pipelines to men didn't work either: It was not considered good form to join a political organization, since objectivity is considered good form on your above-ground newspaper; and I had neither the time nor the inclination to sign up for courses at the university. I had worked my way through college, juggling courses and jobs and putting out the school daily, and had been looking forward to the time when all my energies could go into a job I cared about. And since I was ambitious, I let my job take over most of my waking time; Brian was a part of that too.

We talked about things other than work of course, like the situation in Rhodesia and Polanski movies and Hemingway, but it seems we spent hours each day talking about the joys and frustrations of our work. His story, my story. Gossip around town and on the newspaper. He would critique my stories. Praise them when they were good, make me rewrite when they weren't. He was perfect for someone who told herself nightly that her career came first, nothing would get in her way, and wouldn't it be nice if somehow, someday, she got married—but what about kids? and anyway, think about that some other time.

Brian and I went on like this for months. We stopped having dinner at Billy's because we wanted to be alone, and because we didn't want to arouse anyone's suspicions. Of course we already had, but we didn't want to admit that, or admit to ourselves what was becoming obvious to everyone else. I had become Brian's girl. He picked up my dinner check, and I let him. It felt right. No, it felt wonderful; it was our acknowledgment of an ancient ritual: Man will provide for women. Because she is busy with babies, the rest of it goes. But in the free fall of love, such fine points are immaterial.

One afternoon I was sent to interview the wife of an old Italian. The old man had gone home to visit his native Sicily one last time, but he never got there. A car crashed into him as he was crossing the street at the Rome airport. The newspaper had been wired the story by UPI, and I was dispatched to interview the widow. I couldn't imagine what I was going to ask her, and when I got there, I learned that she didn't even know her husband was dead. She was grocery shopping, her kids said, but I could wait for her. She arrived, all smiles and pushing a shopping cart full of groceries. She assumed that I had come to interview her because her husband was a bigwig with the local Italian social club. We had a hard time communicating because she too was from the old country. I decided, story or not, I was not going to break the news to her. But I hung around for a while, trying to figure out what I could tell the city editor when I got back with my secret intact. She made espresso. Fifteen minutes later, the doorbell rang. Western Union. Now she knew why I had come. The telegram told her. She collapsed into my arms, a bundle of grieving tendons. I signed for the telegram. And I held her, and we wept together. I left when some neighbors arrived, summoned by the children. My story began: "Giovanni Bascali went home to die. . . ."

You stay tuned in when you're a reporter. People might think that sometimes we should leave others alone with their tragedies, but the everyday reporting of such events keeps our ears to the ground to feel the rhythm. Later, after the first edition was out with my story plastered six columns across the top of the second front, I relived it all with Brian.

Was there time to think of where we were going? Did we want to? I knew I wanted to work on a bigger newspaper, that's all.

Back in bed, Brian was still impotent. I was not bothered by this too much, except that he felt terrible, because not going all the way was somehow not so sinful. Don't ask me to explain the logic therein because there isn't any. At least I didn't have to worry about pregnancy, I told myself. I am sure this all sounds terribly old-fashioned and quaint; it was, in fact, only a dozen years ago, but that's how I was: born in the forties, raised in the fifties, when the world was still divided between women who did and women who didn't. Because it was now the sixties and lots of younger women seemed to be handling their sex life as if they had a right to one, did not mean that I could change by fiat. I might have wanted to, I might have wanted to be smart and sophisticated and act like I knew what the world was all about, but inside, I was at war over the fact that I secretly believed that I shouldn't do *it* outside of marriage. I had made that vow to myself once and kept it all through college. A year isn't a long time to turn back a lifetime, and Brian's impotence gave me a chance to breathe and chart a new course. When Brian was ready, I would sleep with him because that's how life was now, because the odds were that we would never get married, and because I wanted to.

When did I decide the old rules no longer made sense? When I didn't marry the boy back home. John and I went together on and off during college, and we should have graduated together, but he got behind—flunking out here, changing schools there. I finished on time, picking up some awards along the way, and took a job in the women's department of *The Saginaw News*. I moved out of my parents' home and took an apartment of my own. John had a miserable civil service job in Flint; he would finish college later.

John showed up one hot Friday night toward the end of June when I was leaving the office. He was waiting in the parking lot to tell me he wanted to get married, right away.

But the magic was gone.

It was clear to me that if I stayed with him, I'd end up in a small Michigan town. I already was in one, and I wanted out. He was going to write fiction and teach in a university while I ate up the newspaper columns in, say, Chicago. We were going to have a sports car and we were going to have Japanese accents in our home and we were going to have kids, at least one.

We were so right once.

There was the time when we were alone in my aunt's house at Christmas, and John came upstairs and we talked while I got ready to go to a party with him. We talked through the eye shadow and perfume, and I felt so feminine, so secure. He was going to be the only man I'd ever want. He had let me believe that it was fine to be both female and ambitious. Others always made me feel that something was wrong, I didn't fit.

But memory is not enough. I'd be trapped behind a white picket fence if I stayed with him. He's going to say something any minute now which smacks of dependency, and I'll wince inside.

But lovers are always dependent, that's what makes them lovers.

But he is no longer off building his own bridges to leave me room for mine.

Will I ever love again as I loved him?

No, because nothing is ever the same again.

Tell me, how does something so fine get lost?

Will there ever be another love? I wanted to tell myself, yes, of course, but there's always the lingering doubt that the one who got away is the only one there will ever be. Life is too chancy for more than an unqualified maybe.

"Let's wait to see what happens," I said. "I just can't marry you now."

"I'll be back in a few days," he said. "On the Fourth of July."

The day was hot and sunny. I got up in the morning

and bathed and washed my hair and splashed myself in lemon cologne. I fixed a picnic lunch of roast chicken and avocado salad and a bottle of white wine. And I waited.

It was one of those times when it is impossible to do anything except wait and feel the seconds crawl by like ticks. There was a porch in front of the house where my apartment was, and there I sat. Swinging. Hour after hour. Trying to read, trying to write in my diary, cursing myself because I was wasting so much time, letting time be my total master. There wasn't much traffic on the street that day, and the sound of any car coming gave me a rush. By sunset, I knew he wasn't coming.

And I knew that I would look for love again. I did not do so well alone. Something hungry rattled through my nights. I would always take a chance, I would always risk the burn at the center of the sun.

In February, I left Michigan. I go back home to visit.

I sailed straight into Brian's arms. He was a wonderful man with whom to have a romance. I am talking about the minutia that transforms an ordinary affair into a passion that will always be so well remembered, no matter the outcome.

If Brian was coming over for dinner on Friday, I spent the day getting ready. Friday was one of my days off. Of course I was wooing him and of course we ate by candlelight. Maybe a simple lamb curry and saffron rice, made with the saffron I'd spent two hours running around to find. Vichyssoise to start—from scratch, naturally. Chocolate mousse pie in a meringue crust for the finish. I learned how to cook from a book.

I planned what I would wear carefully. Six outfits would go on and off before the right one was found. I learned how to make Brian's Gordon's gin martinis, stirred not shaken, the way he liked them. I learned to like Gordon's gin martinis straight up, the way he took his. One time he walked in when Dinah Washington was singing "What a Difference a Day Makes" on the stereo. "Would you like to dance?" were his first words. The next time he came over, he brought a collection of Billie Holiday records and taught me to pay attention to the way Lester Young talks with his horn, he tells the whole sad story with his horn, Brian would say. I never play those records without seeing Brian's face, if only for a second. It's one of those things time dulls but cannot do away with completely.

We didn't always hide in my apartment. Other Friday nights we had dinner out. Our favorite place had red tablecloths and red water goblets and real crystal wine glasses and a red rose in a silver vase on each table. It was where the elegant gays and rich widows gathered, and we knew it was unlikely that we would see people we knew. My favorite outfit—Brian's too—was what used to be called a cocktail dress, slim, scoop-necked and black. I wore a crystal necklace and velvet slippers with sky-high heels, and Brian never forgot to tell me that I looked beautiful. We knew our parts well. You don't need a lot of practice.

Brian would call in the middle of the night, after his wife was surely sleeping, and we would talk for an hour, maybe longer. It got to the point where I would wake up a minute before the first ring.

We sent each other notes at work, love letters stuck in each other's mailboxes, or simple recitations of fact, such as what time the other was expected back at the office, whether it looked like we could have dinner together, as usual, at the usual place. We had long ago abandoned Billy's and instead went to another place near the office where the rest of the crowd came only occasionally. We made a point of leaving the office separately, and when we would call each other on the interoffice phone, even though we sat across the aisle, Brian would make me hang up first, and he would stay on the line, chattering to a void. No one was supposed to notice we had been speaking to one another. Such subterfuge does add a fine tuning to the senses and emotions, turning illicit love into grand passion.

Because you don't have enough time together, every meeting has its ending scheduled as you say, Hello, how are you? and the knowledge of that lurks in the air, regardless how you try to dismiss it. There is an added edge to the moment, whether it's a weekend long or a fifteen-minute cup of coffee at the corner drugstore on Saturday morning. We shouldn't be here in the first place, and in the second place, either one of us can walk out without prior notice. That's one of the rules of any affair; but since we are here, and since we are both loving each other, let us make this time together so special that we will part knowing it has all been worthwhile.

"Brian, I love you. That's it. You don't have to say it back. You make me glad because you are alive and I'm happy to know you and no matter what happens, know that I love you."

"Oh, darlin' . . ."

Of course he can't say it back. He is tied down with a family and doesn't feel he has the right to love me, to make me think that someday we might . . . pull down the shade. Don't think about that. He has a wife. I do not want to be a home wrecker.

He said he was concerned about the inequality of the affair: He had his wife and kids, and as long as I had him, husband hunting I wasn't. I can't quite say I didn't think about it, because I was beginning to imagine what it would be like to be Mrs. Brian McCarthy, and it seemed just fine. But what I said was, I know what I am doing, don't worry about me, I'll take care of myself, this is worth it. I can't say Brian didn't warn me, but then I was not necessarily rational.

Brian never brought up the subject again. To prove my point, I stopped seeing anybody else, while before I might have accepted an occasional date. He didn't want me to, and I felt comfortable and protected by his possessiveness. Without some jealousy, is there love? Besides, other men made me check my wristwatch all evening, wondering when I could politely excuse myself and my God, I hope they don't make a pass.

What did I do Saturday nights? Try not to think about it. I went to the movies with Julie, the lone woman cityside on the other newspaper in town.

In June, Brian was to cover a GOP political dinner in New York City; I got someone else to work in my place, and Brian and I had our first trip out of town. Everything was planned so that no one would connect the two of us. I would take an early flight down and wait for Brian at the hotel, most decidedly not the one where the Republicans would be staying.

Except that the flight I took was the same one booked by the Republican contingent from town; and the county chairman, charming and chatty, sat down next to me, and said, well, now just who are you? There was no point in saying that I was anything other than Girl Reporter, because the next thing I'd know, I would be interviewing him back home about sewage. How interesting, was what he said. Did I know Brian McCarthy was covering their dinner? Why was I going to New York City midweek? Where was I staying? Could he buy me a drink during the next few days? Did I want a ride to town in their limo?

Listen, I'm going to New York City to have an illicit few days with my married lover, with whom you will soon be rubbing shoulders. "I have a friend meeting me in the city. Thank you, but I'll take the bus."

I had a few hours to kill after I checked into the hotel as Mrs. Brian McCarthy (what if they ask for identification, I thought, sweating in my summer sleeves) and so I decided, it being a Wednesday, I would take in a Broadway matinee. *Any Wednesday*, that hilarious comedy about a single woman who only sees her married lover midweek, was what I chose. Much to my chagrin, I found myself laughing.

By the time Brian and I left New York, he was no longer impotent with me. And I was fast losing interest in keeping our secret. I was ready to start shouting it from the rooftops.

Now that Brian and I knew each other in the Biblical sense, I had to admit to myself that I was doing what I was doing. It was as easy as getting dressed in the morning. Yet to face a stranger and ask for birth control pills? What happened in the bedroom and what one admitted were not the same in those days. Would I lie to the doctor and make up a married name? Would I be brazen and cool, a modern woman? Would I wear a wedding band and say nothing? Nothing is what I did. We relied on the rhythm method and withdrawal for a few months, both of which everyone knows are highly unreliable.

Tomorrow, I would say to myself, tomorrow I will go to a doctor. I will open the phone book and choose one. Brian didn't use condoms, probably because they are so unappealing. My inability to act may have been an unconscious way of forcing the hand to be played, regardless of the consequences. Not doing anything is, after all, doing something. It may not allow for much control over your life and it leaves you the victim of circumstance, but events catch up and the weather changes, and there's always a part of you deep down that knows you did what you thought you had to, for the best of reasons, for the worst of reasons. In my case, it was one of those times when the situation had to get worse before life could get better.

"Darlin', we're rare."

We had stolen away from the office at dinnertime and had come back to my apartment. I was lying in his arms on my rollaway bed.

"Oh, no, lots of people fall in love this much. . . ."

"No, we're rare. Trust me."

I disagreed again, insisting that lots of people find this kind of connection, but Brian said no, and I could tell he was gettting annoyed, and besides, it was nice to be in the arms of a man who believed he loved you so much that this love set us apart from other lovers.

"I know that in ten years from now, I could call you from some airport, and you would come to meet me."

Call me from an airport? I know what we agreed to in the beginning, but everything's changed. I might even change my name to his, if he would ask, and that's something I never thought I would do. I want to spend the rest of my life with this man, and he is talking about ten years from now at an airport, two people having a gin martini in the bar, two people looking for threads?

I have no right to go back on our bargain, to cry and complain, but I didn't know it would come to this, I hadn't counted on love.

We bought each other a lot of presents those months, and if some of Brian's were given out of guilt because he couldn't give himself, I didn't care. Lovely presents, they were: cameo earrings to go with the antique pin from my father, a silver bud vase, a lighter like his, inscribed with the letter *l* in lowercase script, the way I sign my name, books he wanted me to read: *Appointment in Samarra, Watch Your Language,* by an editor of *The New York Times.* I gave him silk ties and a biography of Hemingway.

Brian spent the best part of his tenth wedding anniversary with me. He and the wife were going out to dinner, and I was giving a party to avoid thinking about that. He called around midnight. There had been a fight, he had taken Kathleen home and was in a bar. I got rid of everybody in the next hour or so and waited. Somewhere around four or five, after we had made love and were lying in the afterglow, he said, at first in a voice that I had to strain to hear, "I'll come to you. Just be patient. I know tonight I'll come to you." It was the Fourth of July and the fireworks were going off inside me.

Dawn came and he left. Too excited to sleep, I sat up in a chair, a funny straw one, smoked cigarettes and listened to Billie Holiday. I would get to have both work and love. I thought it was quite surprising. Amazing, in fact.

On Saturdays, when he worked and I didn't, we would often meet for coffee at a drugstore before he went to the office. And then, a few hours later, I frequently would stop in the office on the pretext of getting my mail or checking over a story running the next day. I just happened to be downtown, I said. And I would have lunch with Brian and Owen, who was my boss, and maybe another reporter, and we would all act as if nothing were going on between Brian and me.

Those lunches also gave me a chance to spring new story ideas on Owen. I got to cover serious beats only on the regular reporter's day off. I was always getting these nutty assignments thought up because I was a woman. What do single women do at night? for instance. On top of everything else, the editor in charge on Owen's days off, which amounted to nearly half my work week, was of the old school. A woman in the city room? You've got to be kidding. He assigned me obits and rewrites of publicity handouts, no matter what. Except for the time when he thought covering a Rolling Stones concert might as well go to the Girl. There turned out to be a disturbance; the police stopped the performance as Mick Jagger started taking off his shirt; the kids went wild; and the story ended up on the Associated Press wire. Other than that, I can't remember ever getting good assignments from him.

Owen was better, but he once sent me out to get an undercover job as a go-go dancer. The joint was a hangout of the Mob. Naturally I was enthusiastic about the story and pleased when I was hired on merit. It's always made a good story in the telling, but I met no mobsters, I only worked one night, and my story never ran, which is probably what upset me the most. To get that next job on a bigger paper, I needed to be taken seriously. I know I was just paying my dues, but I was impatient to get on with it, and I was tired of having to jump through a hoop because I was a woman.

Eventually, Brian told Owen about us. Owen said, I already know, everyone does. I was pleased; going public, at least this little bit, made our love less of a scandal somehow, and after all, if he could tell his best friend, could The Wife be far behind?

I am quite sure I know the time the child was conceived. There is nothing to back that up, naturally, but a certain feeling, and that will do.

It was a time that was not likely to be safe, and I think I mentioned this to Brian at the beginning, so that he would pull away before he came, but by the time we were in the middle of making love, there was so much flowing back

and forth with eyes wide open and the sun going down outside the window where hung bits of colored glass, making
patches of rainbow on the floor. I remember I noticed the
beads of sweat on Brian's chest, how blue were his eyes. I
felt as if he were looking right through me and loving
everything he saw and touched, and I also knew I could
not tell him to stop. There had been too much trouble over
tears and guilt, months of impotency, and I would not say
anything to upset this delicate balance. I just thought,
please, don't make me pregnant, it took my mother two
years to have me, and you're not going to make me pregnant so fast, are you? I guess it comes down to the fact
that a woman always knows she can conceive, and her
life will be forever changed after that if she does, and so
even in the hot spots of passion there is a certain detached
awareness of what might happen afterward.

When my period was a few days late, I had no
trouble finding a doctor. Called up the medical society and
went to the first one they recommended. He was as cold
and plastic as his office while I nervously spilled out my
story of how I was going with a law student and we couldn't
get married now, we simply couldn't. What I was trying to
convey was, if I am indeed pregnant, will you please do
an abortion? Or send me somewhere I can have one?
Confronted with the fact that I might actually have a
child growing inside me, the admonitions of the Church
blew away like so many scraps of the Baltimore catechism.

But the next day brought the good news: The test was
negative. Brian and I had champagne at our favorite
restaurant. I had a prescription for birth control pills. I
could start taking them as soon as I had a period.

Brian and I would sometimes meet in the park where
I went horseback riding for an hour or so on Sundays, when

he could slip away. He said he would come to me, and I repeated those words like a litany.

His wife said nothing, nothing about the weeks that had stretched into months since they had made love, nothing about the more and more time he was spending "with the guys," nothing about what I presumed was the growing distance between them. All I could think was that she didn't want to admit what was happening, or she knew but didn't care, or didn't want to confront Brian. He was waiting for her to walk away, and there was really no way I could precipitate that. I learned patience in the face of pain, and I got presents from Brian as rewards.

Brian and I were getting more reckless, daring fate to carry the news back to his wife. If only she would have made an ugly scene, he could have walked away, more or less gracefully. Yet such good-byes are seldom graceful, for in relationships when content is everything, style counts for nothing. Anyway, the night of the Newspaper Guild's Page One Show and party afterward, Brian and I were obviously a couple; she had declined to come. We even went in Brian's car, and as we walked in together, we ran smack into the Republican County Chairman, my seatmate on the plane to New York City months earlier.

Brian's wife did attend a going-away party for a reporter moving to Washington. I was there too, it couldn't be avoided. But her path and mine didn't cross all evening. No one would tell her about us, but one of the wives got hold of Brian: Why are you taking chances like this? She's a good woman, a good mother, think about what you are risking.

Brian and I talked vaguely about moving to another city one day. Yes, Brian, I'll wait, but how long? How many more nights will you get up and leave me with your sperm running down my legs and crushed empty packs of Luckies in the living room and Billie Holiday singing "I know our love will linger when the other love forgets, so I say good-bye with no regrets. . . ."

I had a period, sort of. Faint red streaking, not unusual for me. A tendency toward anemia does that. I started taking the pills religiously. I telephoned the doctor, told him I actually hadn't bled buckets, and asked would he care to see me, just to make sure?"

No. No need for that.

I had another period, sort of. Still the doctor didn't want to see me. I took another month's worth of pills.

Did I know I was pregnant? I don't believe so, even today. Uncertain, maybe. Yes, that's right, uncertain. How long would Brian and I be together? A lifetime, like he said? Or would he give his love and then take it back? Did he love me enough to do what he said he wanted to do, come and claim me in front of the world? He called me his woman. Would I ever be wife?

I started throwing up in the morning and afternoon. I told myself it was the flu or a nervous stomach. I did not gain any weight, but then I was always dieting. I did not notice any particular changes in the shape of my body or my breasts, and neither did Brian. It still amazes me what you can do with your body, when you put your mind to it. By denying that I was with child, I was keeping it under wraps, as it were, while I waited for Brian to do something. He kept saying he would, please just wait a little longer, I can't do it yet. As long as I wasn't pregnant, we could go on in the present, and live on our love from day to day. Caught between belief and doubt, hope and despair, illusion was a comforting solution, however transitory: I am not pregnant, I am not pregnant, the doctor told me so.

I went home for Christmas. I had not seen my family since February, when they had watched their only daughter move east. They had not put up a hue and cry then, they had done that earlier when I first moved out of the house, after I graduated from college. It was not in my mother's frame of reference to have a daughter leave home unless she had a husband waiting.

She asked if I was dating anyone special. No.

An old boyfriend from college came over and brought a present of costume jewelry and the news that he was about to become engaged.

My mother said I seemed more nervous and high strung than usual. We had a hard time talking, but then we usually had a hard time talking. I knew I hadn't turned out to be the kind of daughter she had been, the kind of daughter she had wanted, the kind of daughter who had a white wedding in church. "Lorraine, are you sure you're doing the right thing? A career isn't everything, you know. Are you going to be happy?"

"I'm doing the only thing I can, Mother." I know I am such a disappointment.

On January 3 I got back from Dearborn. I looked at my stomach, I looked at my breasts, telephoned the doctor and insisted he see me that afternoon.

"You are close to five months pregnant," he said icily as he fingered me inside. "The tests must have been wrong. It's not one hundred percent accurate in the early stages of pregnancy."

I telephoned Brian at the office—I hadn't seen him

since I got back—and blurted out my news. He said we would talk later. I dressed and went to work.

That afternoon, the best assignment I'd ever had was handed to me. I was to go down to Columbus, where the First Cavalry was based, the First Cavalry that had lost so many men in Vietnam, and interview the widow of a local man, and do a mood piece of the town, where many widows continued to live. The chief photographer would come down on the last day. Do not think about yourself. Do the job, and do it well. "Jay used to say that we had more happiness in seven years than most people have in a lifetime," she had said, and that's how I ended the story.

I must get an abortion. Brian is supposed to be arranging it while I am here. This is much too stupid to be happening to me, this is a script from the afternoon soaps: Daughter who thinks she knows all moves away from home to live in sin in distant city; she gets her comeuppance. The nuns and priests are in the audience. Fade out.

Abortion. Today there are billboards advertising them, subway signs in Spanish, listings in the Yellow Pages and advertisements in *The Village Voice*. In 1966, at least where I lived, abortion was still a whispered word. I have since read how people got them back then. Women went to expensive doctors and expensive hospitals in New York City and paid their money and two psychiatrists agreed that something desperate might be done (suicide? gin and wire coat hangers? hot baths and falling off horses? hurling yourself down a flight of stairs?) if the abortion was not. But I didn't know about that, and neither did Brian.

I ended up in Puerto Rico a week later with a thousand dollars in traveler's checks, and the name of five people who might be able to help. The names were given to Brian by the Puerto Rican secretary of the man who lent Brian the money. The first person on the list was the woman's sister, who knew I was coming. I had taken a cab out to her neat stucco house in the suburbs. Her two young children were there, but they did not understand English.

"You certainly don't look pregnant," she said for openers. Then: "Why don't you stay here and have the child and I will raise it for you?"

I still wonder about that. But a child anywhere is a responsibility for life. "I can't do that. But will you help me find a doctor, one who will give me an abortion?"

"I don't know why you people think it is so easy here," she replied. "It's against the law, and I don't know anyone."

The next three people on the list could not be tracked down: A motel manager and a dining room captain had moved on, and the third number had been disconnected. The woman and a friend came to see me at the hotel. They had the name of a doctor. I telephoned. He was on vacation for three weeks. My last chance—before I asked the hookers in the Condado section—was an attorney who put me in touch with the right kind of doctor.

At 8 A.M. the next morning, his waiting room was full of pregnant Puerto Rican women, who stared at the American who did not look with child. I assumed they all knew why I was there. I had assumed that the cabdriver knew why he was taking me to this doctor. Didn't he look at me funny when I paid him?

The nurse took me out of order, calling my name ten minutes after I walked in.

And then I was up on his table and my legs were in

the hated stirrups. If there is a time I wish my genitalia were external, it is the time of an internal examination.

How many doctors have poked around inside me? Felt my insides and gone this way and that? A regular procession that got started when I was twelve and my period started and then stopped and then started again, but this time it didn't stop. Doctor A, this is Exhibit Lorraine. Most unusual case. Terminal bleeding. Do you think something is wrong with her head that she can't shut off the blood? What would a soothsayer say? Doctor B, Meet Specimen Lorraine. Young she is, give her another pill, give her another test, shoot her up with hormones, whambam, isn't this one brave, she does not cry, she does not blink, she does not go tight and tense while we keep roaming around with plastic gloves and mechanical fingers. Look she has blonde hair, just peach fuzz. I always hated it. *Tell me doctor, tell me now that it is not too late.* Tell me with the thick lips and the black moustache. *You can have me if you want, I will not make a sound, it happened to a friend once and I got goose bumps when she told me, but I will not report you to the authorities.* So different when it is Brian's finger, so different when it feels nice. Was it like this at Auschwitz? Finally, when I was thirteen and through two-dozen doctors and as many fingers, an operation. A simple D & C, it fixèd me up fine. *Please doctor, that is all I want now, it is not too late, this is going to ruin my life if it is too late. Why am I the woman?*

"You are five months pregnant. I cannot do anything. It is too dangerous."

"NO! It can't be too late . . . I don't care what happens, please do it."

"It is too late. You might die."

"I don't care—if this happens—it can't."

"You might die. I will not do it."

"Please, please . . ."

"That is ten dollars."

I took the 11 A.M. flight home. I can hear my mother's voice at the top of her lungs: You are no better than a whore! College graduate? What did they teach you there? How to get pregnant? All your fancy talk about getting a job on a newspaper and look what happens to you! I knew you would come to no good when you said you wanted to leave home! How could you do this to me? How could you go to mass at Christmas?

A letter had been waiting for me when I got back to the hotel. I read it again and again. The letter was written on the fourteenth, marking an anniversary of the first time we were together. Brian described the snowflakes falling outside the windows in contrast to me high above the Atlantic somewhere. He told me what time it was, and he told me that Owen had just said, "Dusky's story from Georgia is great, and I'm spreading it all over the Sunday paper." There would be a promotion teaser with photographs running in the Saturday edition. Brian told me that he thought about me constantly, all day, imagined what I was doing every minute, every hour, and that when he was not doing that he remembered how I looked and what I said the night before.

I wondered what specifically I had said. *In the shadow past the pain, will love ever be reclaimed?* No, but I noted that crisis does call to life the latent poet.

Brian wrote the letter in two parts, continuing the next day. He stayed up late that night listening to Lady Day and Lester Young, smoking cigarettes and sipping Four Roses, "thinking about a blonde girl and a green island."

What had I done the night before? Had dinner with

an attractive young banker from Montreal who was staying in my hotel. It was bloody awful and it was better than being alone.

Brian said it was snowing again. Everything around him was natural and normal, but only it wasn't. He was about to go to lunch with Owen and a few of the other reporters. He said he was worried and anxious but not frightened, because he remembered how brave I was. He had a million questions to ask me and he knew that I would soon answer all of them.

There are pictures in the heart that cannot be conveyed in mere words. Brian will never quite understand about this child and the way that I would know this child, no matter what words I use or how long I speak.

He signed off saying that he loved me, he was thinking of me every minute.

I looked out the window. It was that blank gray you see when you are in the middle of a cloud. The color is dull, lifeless, and holds no promise.

I cannot have this child. I said it out loud to Brian when he picked me up at the airport, as if making the statement were some kind of answer in itself. I said it in the car, I said it later at my apartment when Brian's arms enfolded me, holding me close and keeping the devils at bay for a few hours. Then he had to go home.

"It will be soon, darlin'. I'll come to you."

I smile through the tears, through hot puffy eyes that burn. I go to the window and watch him get in his car and drive away.

I cannot believe all my carefully wrought plans are being blown away by biology. I did everything I was supposed to: editor of high school paper, column in hometown weekly when I was sixteen, summer jobs as a reporter, managing editor of college daily, journalism scholarship, awards, straight A's in writing courses. I always knew I had to do more to stay even.

And now, pregnant. That's the part that's off the graph.

I did not learn that along with piling up those qualifications that have no sex, I should have found some way to neutralize the fact that I was born female. I was so intent on ignoring it, I did not learn how to manage it. Instead, I went around for years saying I wish I had been born a man. So neat, so simple do their lives seem. "What did you have, Charlie? Boy or girl? Well, let's see about that bonus."

I sat through job interview after job interview assuring The Man that I was not planning on getting married, not planning on having a child. What I should have been doing was seeing a doctor. I had been so careful about everything else.

A doctor could have sewn up my genitals, but he couldn't reach inside and reset the genes, turn back the programming. What did I do when I finally had the job I wanted? Went out and fell in love with the first man who came along. Just like a woman. And now I wanted to marry him.

Before the world catches on how smooth my female parts are working, I will have to leave the job. Go into hiding, I suppose, have this child, and . . . oh my God, I cannot yet face that.

I couldn't imagine how I was going to piece my life back together when all this was over, I couldn't imagine admitting to my parents back home in Michigan how I'd botched up my life, I couldn't imagine calling an adoption agency and I couldn't imagine not calling one. I couldn't imagine anything it seems, except what a shoddy mess I'd made of everything, how unfair it was to be the woman.

That thing inside my belly? Not a real living thing. Not with feelings you had to consider.

Suicide seemed like the most reasonable alternative, but I never got around to it. Maybe I wasn't serious, because I never once actually tried it, and even as I was figuring out how, I was talking myself out of it.

Brian kept his job and paid my rent and bought our groceries.

In the mornings, I read *The New York Times* as if I were preparing for a test. I would look out the window down onto the street three stories below and watch pregnant women and mothers attached to buggies and strollers march by; I think they must have been having a conference in my neighborhood, so many of them there were. In the afternoons, I cooked dinner for us. Brian called at least two or three times a day. By the time I heard him coming up the steps I was all clean hair and lipstick and perfume, ready to discuss a global crisis somewhere.

One day Brian told me the reporter from Michigan I had recommended for a job had arrived to start work; he was told that I was back in Michigan tending a dying father, that was the official story. He shook his head in surprise; why only weeks ago, I'd had him up for drinks and lobster bisque when he came to town for his tryout.

One day Brian arrived with the name and phone number of a local adoption agency. I put the paper away, but in a safe place.

I continued to hope that maybe Brian would come to me now, while there was still time, and then we could keep the child and get married when he was free and live happily ever after. But even as I spoke I could sense how pointless were my pleas.

He said he just couldn't come now. He said it lots of ways different ways, and yet there were days when something in his words let me have the faintest of hope that maybe he would find the strength to claim me now, while I was carrying his baby, our love child. But then another week would have slipped by and nothing would have happened except that I would have learned a new recipe or two and got five more rows along on the petit point evening bag I had begun stitching.

"I'll come to you, Lorraine. I just can't right now, I can't leave the kids yet. Please don't think less of me. I love you and I know I want to be with you."

And baby makes three?

"It will be better if we have the child adopted, and then later we can start off together somewhere. It won't be easy, there will be alimony and child support, but we'll be OK. But wait. Please wait."

By the time he got to the part about adoption, I was fighting tears, usually a futile endeavor. I've always cried easily, and now was not the time to learn anything different.

As the weeks drifted by, the baby inside me sprang to life. No, I wouldn't kill myself. I remember I read somewhere that pregnant women actually have one of the lowest rates of suicide, and now I understood why. Even in the darkest of moments, there was something quite wonderful about the new life stirring in my womb.

I got books from the library on how to take care of the child inside me, and eventually, it took over my consciousness. I made sure that I got plenty of fresh air, and I drank milk even though I don't like it. I didn't forget to take the special vitamins the doctor gave me. Not ever.

And the baby, now rounding me out, now pushing past the waistlines of my clothes, now changing my life irrevocably in ways I did not yet fully comprehend, gave validity to the love between Brian and me. No longer could we ever be just another tawdry affair, no matter what anyone said or thought, for our child would be living, breathing proof of our love and our time together for as long as the world existed, regardless of what happened to Brian and me, regardless of how our lives would turn out.

It seems funny to say it, but there were lots of times when I was proud to be with child.

"Can I fix you a martini?" Brian would ask.

"No, I've switched to tomato juice. Less calories, more nutritious."

"Darlin' I love you, you're so brave."

Hahahahahaha.

3

Letter to an Unborn Child

I tried to kill you, but I do not hate you. I looked for a doctor who would take a sharp knife and scrape you away into nothingness. I would have been put to sleep with you living in me, and a short time later the nurse would wake me, and you would be gone, dead before you ever really lived.

Now it is weeks later, and I feel you more every day. You kick me, you cause hard bulges in my stomach, you do not let me sleep for more than a few hours at a time. Sometimes I think you are standing on your hands kicking your feet against the wall of my stomach. I know you are not doing that, but I like to think that you are.

You will be born in a few months, and now my shape is changing more every day. Perhaps if you would have made yourself noticeable sooner, you would have died. I would have had the abortion. I think so. Perhaps you knew that all along, and that is why you didn't make me look different, not even under the scrutiny of your father when he saw me naked. I could not see you myself for months when I stood nude in front of the mirror on the bedroom door. But now you kick and jab as if to kid me about having been there all along.

Now that you have announced your presence, I cannot help but love you, because you are me and you are him. But I have to admit, there are times I still wish you would die, because if you were dead, I would at least know what had happened to you. There are so many things to tell you, and I will set them down here, and someday try to get this to you. I will worry about *how* later.

If you did not live, you would never have to know the hurt and disappointment of a friend's betrayal. You would never have to know the inside ache when a trust is misplaced, when a secret you thought was safe from the world turns up in the oddest place to haunt you, to hurt you. You would never have to feel as if you were on the outside of a glass window and everybody inside was having a good time, and nobody was waving for you to come on in.

I remember when I was in the second grade and took a packet of valentines to school. I had at least thirty. We all put our valentines in a big box that someone had decorated with red hearts and red and white ribbons and lacy paper doilies, and just before school was over for the day, the teacher appointed a few students to pass out the valentines. I remember waiting and waiting and only getting two valentines. Now that I am older I can sometimes tell the story and laugh, but I really do not think it is funny. I was seven then, and on that day I suffered as much as I could.

When we grow older, the things that hurt us are different and they seem larger than the pains of childhood.

But I am not sure they are different, in the feelings, I mean. We all get what we can handle. It is up to us to make the most of the life that is ours. Giving you away is testing my outer limits. There are times I am not sure I will endure. I would rather be facing sure death. I could cry, moan and scream Why me? but at least I would be looking forward to a time when everything would be over, the pain would cease, the cares about which my mind troubles simply end. But I cannot think about the easy way out, I must think about the fact that you are going to live, that I am not going to do anything to endanger that, and that I am going to do everything I can to make you healthy. I would try to make you wealthy and wise, if I could.

But I seem to be rambling on about the bad parts, and there's a lot more to life than that. Yes, there are disappointments, but there is also beauty and grace and the sheer wonder of them all. There is the clean feeling of diving into a smooth clear blue lake and maybe swimming by the fish as they swim away, there is the serenity of a beautiful thought, there is the joy of simply breathing when you are alone on a galloping horse by the sea and the sun is dropping down into a wide slice of ocean.

There is the tranquillity and excitement of being in love, the well-being that comes from having a trusted friend, the pleasure of making a child smile, the singular beauty of a rose right after the rain, or a garden in which you can see forever, or at least tomorrow. There is the snap of a crisp green apple, the feeling of hot sand on bare feet, the rush of jumping out of an airplane and watching your parachute blossom right in front of your eyes. There are these things, and so many more.

But to see and know the good parts of life, you will have to suffer through some of the bad, because if you do not, you will not be capable of the understanding and compassion that are important. I hope you decide the good outweigh the bad. Times when I didn't. I do now. Maybe it is because I am bringing forth new life, I am bringing forth you.

Life is good and bad and glorious and tedious and sad and happy, but most of all, it's change. Perhaps this is all we can ever be sure of: that the weather changes. Sometimes you just have to sit it out, wait for the bad parts to blow away. But be aware that the bad parts, the hard knocks, these are what teach you, there's no way around that. When you look back, you will think, yes, that is when I learned such and such.

You'll look around sometimes and you'll see that other lives seem easier, a little gentler on the mind: Why am I adopted? you'll ask. Try to think only that you have got to learn more than others because you have more to do passing through. Don't ask why. Such things just are.

But I have to admit that being philosophical doesn't help much when you're hurting. I guess I am trying to say that since we can't do anything about the pain, we might as well try to make some good out of it.

Our separation is not going to be easy on either of us. I have to give you away and you have to be given away. Oh baby, I wish it didn't have to be that way. Afterward, both of us will always be different from most of the rest. There will be a mark deep inside that only you and I know about. Only you and I know how it feels. I know you didn't ask to be born a bastard, and if I could have chosen, I wouldn't have been born female. All we can do is make do.

You have been through so much already I do not even question whether or not you are going to make it. If you had not been meant to live, you would have died when I fell off that horse, when I dove over and over into a swimming pool, when I ran for a mile in the early morning sun. If you had been meant to die, you would have done it finally on a doctor's table. But he said no to me and yes to you.

Baby, you kick me, and there is so much that I want to tell you, but know that I never can. I will never even know how you are called. They tell me I will know whether you are a girl or a boy, and that I may see you if I want to. I do not know if I can stand that, because it would make me love you more than I already do. I wonder what you will look like and if you will have hay fever and long arms like me. I wonder if your nose will be too big and if your hair will be blonde like mine and your father's, and if you will be tall and rangy the way he is. I wonder if you will like words the way your father and I do; I wonder if you will be a writer. And sometimes I wonder if you will die of leukemia when you are ten. I will never know.

That will always be the hardest part, never knowing what you are like or who you are, what you have become. Perhaps every time I hear about an adopted child your age, I will wonder if it is you. I hope that your family will encourage you to study and like books and music and art. Your father likes jazz, I like ballet. I took lessons as a child and the ballet teacher told my mother I should work hard at it, but I didn't. I took to books instead. But maybe you will be a dancer.

I wish I could tell you all about your family, which stretches back to Poland on your maternal grandmother's side and straight to the court of the last czar of Russia on your maternal grandfather's side and back to Ireland on your father's side. But they tell me I can never tell you these things. That is what the social worker tells me. They have taken all this information down on sheets of paper, and they say they will try to match you as best they can, that the parents will at least be Roman Catholic, but they do not tell me how much you will ever know about your flesh-and-blood heritage. I know you will have another one, but what shall we do with your place in my family tree?

In spite of everything, baby, I don't have any regrets. What would I regret—that I know your father? I cannot regret that because together we are better than we can be when we are alone; he makes it easier to get through the day just because he is alive. You will grow up, and one day you will know what I mean about the love between a man and a woman.

And my child, I am well past the point of regretting that you are to be born.

I am afraid of the time of your birth. For as long as I can remember, I have been afraid of dying when and if I had a baby. I do not think you will kill me, although it would be just. I tried to get rid of you. Now you are going to live. Me too. And we will never know each other. This brief time we have together, with you inside of me, you still part of me, is all the time we will ever have.

You have taught me that it is wonderful to have new life inside me. I will never forget you. I will celebrate your birthdays and your first communion and your graduation from elementary school and your high school prom. This will be our secret.

I hope you will not hate me when you learn about me. Before you could love me or hate me, you would have to know me.

You will know me in your genes. Your body comes from me and it comes from your father, and nothing will ever alter that. If you should ever see me, you would not remember me. But look at your hand. Look at yourself in the mirror. You will see me there. And I hope that somehow my love will be etched there too.

Baby, it is so hard to give you away, but he and I cannot get married now. You were conceived in love. I hope that makes a difference; it is all I can give.

Maybe someday, this fall, next year, five years from now, or when I am old and gray, I will know that I have done the wrong thing in giving you away. But I do not know about next fall or five years from now, I can only do what I think is best now. I cannot keep you.

You're so strong, in my heart I think you are a son. I think life is easier if you are male, and so when we talk about you, we always call you "he" and "him." My son. My son.

Son, there is so much I want to tell you, so much love I want to encircle you with, so much I cannot do for you, so much that must go unsaid.

I tried to kill you, but do not hate me. I love you. I love you. I love you.

Winter gave way to a dull, wet spring. I went for long walks during the day, I read Thomas Wolfe at night after Brian had gone. In April, the sun came.

And then she was born.

4

Labor Pains

I had just thrown an infant down a flight of stairs.

Shrieking unlike anything I'd ever heard before whipped through the air like a hot tornado.

The baby kept slipping farther down toward the blackness at the bottom. And as much as I wanted to leap down and rescue the screaming child, I would not—could not—make myself move. A stronger force, not anything I could see or touch, kept me planted like a statue. I knew the wailing was the sound of a soul in torment, yet I could only weep and listen.

I wake up sweating with the howling floating through the haze.

That damn dream again—every night for a week.

My belly aches. Feels like a menstrual cramp. But baby knows it is too late for that.

Two A.M. Maybe Brian will call. One of his phone

calls in the middle of the night from the library while the wife is asleep upstairs. Brian will be sitting there in the library with Billie Holiday and Four Roses, boozily contemplating Us, and so he'll call. Doesn't he know that isn't good enough anymore? Brian: Hot Shot Political Writer and Weekend Columnist. I'll read you with my morning coffee, but I need you tonight. The bogeymen are out tonight.

I take two aspirins and drift off into a dreamless, arid sleep. Pain goes off like buzzers somewhere around three A.M.

Pain-killers won't work now. Only oblivion holds salvation.

This is not the kind of pain you feel when you burn yourself, the kind that sears in one particular place. This reverberates from within and is held back only by the skin of the stomach. I put my hand on my belly, half-believing the touch will singe my fingers. It doesn't. I feel for hard bulges. There are none. I push down the covers and pull up the T-shirt—one of Brian's—I'm wearing. My stomach looks the same as it had the night before: pink, smooth, a neat arc, a geometric curve. The fire is within. How tidy.

Trying to be brave tonight is absurd. But necessary. I want to wake somebody up and tell him how much I hurt, somehow it won't be so bad then. Hello, baby. We're not much comfort to each other.

Maybe I can read, something light, a Greek tragedy.

I have just messed up my own first act. There I was covering death in the afternoon and rock stars on tour.

But forever female.

And then Bam! Pregnant. Whoever said biology is destiny was right.

I am not one of your super ladies who can rock
a cradle with one hand and type with the other. I have
known I wanted to write since I was ten; I always had
doubts about being somebody's mommy. But I do have
maternal instincts. Giving my baby away is ungluing me.
Will I ever be put right again?

I move from the kitchen through the living room
through the foyer and back into the bedroom as if I am
a guest on tour.

GUEST: That Buffet print is interesting—such a sad
         clown.
ME: My Last Duchess.
GUEST: There are cigarette burns on the carpet.
ME: Brian's cigarettes fall on the floor. We make
         love on a single bed that is poorly disguised
         as a sofa. Which was left behind by the
         Chinese artist who lived here before me. I
         also live on leftover love.
GUEST: How come you keep your typewriter in the
         living room?
ME: That's how I live. And I don't have to walk
         far to the sofa.
GUEST: You brought all these books from Detroit?
         Even your ninth-grade English reader?
ME: I drag my past around with me. I have a
         new book. *Joy of Cooking.*
GUEST: How long are you staying?
ME: Well, the baby's due next month, and then
         . . . Brian says he will leave his wife, but
         he doesn't know when because the guilt
         over three kids and Catholicism is rather

incapacitating. But he loves me, and I don't think I could face going back to the newspaper—if I could—I don't know.

Does being a woman mean I'll always be Silly Putty? It does mean I have a womb.

Why do Brian and I always think it will be a boy? Because it's too hard the other way.

Brian says he is unhappy about giving our child away. Unhappy! This child is a part of me: Baby and me, we make one. This is going to be an amputation.

How will I feel if Brian and I actually end up together, and the kid is gone? Rotten. I guess I know I can't count on him. There's only me, and I cannot keep this child. I was making $130 a week. I need a car for my job. I was working strange hours. Where would I get a baby-sitter? Afford a baby-sitter? And baby needs a father. I'm not strong enough to let the world know that I have an illegitimate child. Movie stars are. I've got a galloping case of Catholic guilt, and somehow my bastard would end up getting spare change. Oh baby inside me, this is a most unnatural act.

I have become a baby machine. For some folks who can't have children of their own but want to change diapers and cuddle babies. So why do I worry about the rent? Why don't I have a doctor of my own, why am I a clinic patient? Why . . . Christ, this really hurts. Fire and pins, pay for your sins: Guilty in the highest degree. Is this going to go on all month and what time is it?

Three thirty-two.

Everybody in the world is sleeping except the man downstairs who coughs and me whining here on a rollaway bed. With a fucking fire in my belly.

Where is the pain precisely? Everything from my

belly button on down is having a migraine. Prometheus
didn't get away with bringing down fire, and I got burned
for playing with it. And now the Furies are making this
whore pay: *You shall be grilled by the sun's bright fire
and change the fair bloom of your skin. . . . Always the
grievous burden of your torture will be there to wear you
down; for he that shall cause it to cease has yet to be born.*

My mother: probably still saying rosaries to stave off
what I have already done. All the Hail Marys in the world
aren't enough to reach from the middle of America to the
eye of this storm. You always knew, didn't you, Mother?
That's why there's the trouble between us.

These aspirins aren't working at all. Hooks gash away
at my insides. Yet my stomach doesn't even shake and this
can't be the baby because the baby's not due for a month
and if I bite my lips will I forget about the torrent down
there? And is this physical pain I'm feeling any worse because I'm such a slut?

I wonder if I have a fever—I'm all hot and sweaty.
This isn't really high grade enough to call an ambulance
and it's too early to call anybody else. Four ten. I'll call
somebody at seven.

Not Brian. Hooray for Brian! You win the paternity
sweepstakes, but we will spare you a phone call. My family
in Detroit? They don't even know. Julie, the only friend in
town who knows my secret? She can't help. I don't want to
bother Mrs. Hera, earth mother of the adoption agency. I
even have her home number, but now is the time to be a
big girl. And if I want a doctor to treat a few lousy stomach
cramps in the middle of the night, I'd have to go to an
emergency room. The world wants its full pound of flesh.

Listen, slut, you have no right to be a smart ass.

When you are trapped by ruin, don't blame fortune. . . .
Your own want of good sense has tangled you in the net
of ruin, past all good fortune.

Two more aspirins and I drift into a half wakefulness broken almost as soon as it begins. A thousand ice picks are digging through the lining of my stomach. I put my hand on my vagina. Medium wet. I get out of bed, drawing the blanket around me. I go into the living room and look out the window.

All quiet on Western Avenue.

More aspirins? But how will they affect the child inside me? Water will do this time. My mouth feels like a dry water hole, my skin a swamp. Like a sleepwalker, I move into the foyer and lie down on the floor, putting the telephone next to me. I take the receiver off the hook and listened to the hum: a lifeline. Four fifty. Too early to telephone and still be a reasonable person.

I shall keep my foulness to myself. If I'd made other choices, I could be sporting a chastity belt, I could be back home in Dearborn playing Scrabble with the folks, I could be married to someone nice. But instead I move to my doom.

Five ten.

It's strange that now I don't even consider suicide. I spent so many years devising different plots for self-destruction, but I never had the guts to carry them through. Like my aunt did.

But killing myself now would be killing the baby.

I didn't worry about that when I went off to Puerto Rico shopping for an abortionist. It was the baby's good fortune to not make his presence known until he was almost five months along: I even had periods. I was thrown off a horse at two months, for Christ's sake. And then

when I finally found the man who would scrape every-
thing away, he said: It is too late. You might die.
I said: I'll take that chance.
He said: I won't. Ten dollars, please.
This is a child who was meant to be born.

Nobody ever told me that it would be like this. I read
all the books on birth I could find in the library, and they
didn't tell me that it would hurt this much. Nobody can
ever really tell you anything, can they? Not even Anne
Frank.

With all the wretchedness I feel, I should break out
in impetigo or boils or leprosy, pus running down my body,
so the world could see my filth. Yet I look in the mirror and
see this sad person with clear eyes and a thin face and
straight long blonde hair and a big nose that looks like it
was pulled off of somebody else's face and glued onto
mine. This person can even smile at the mouth. The eyes
tell you differently; touch me and all the emotional garbage
inside explodes and mucks up the walls, the sky, like some
gigantic boil of corruption come apart. Baby, you know I
don't mean you.

Six ten. A thousand murderous prickle points congeal
inside my stomach. I can't stand this any longer. I am
going to call the agency. "Look, I hate to bother you this
early, but I have an incredible pain in my stomach. The
baby's not due for a month."
"Who is your doctor?"
"I'm a clinic patient, but I've seen Dr. Rawji almost
every time I went for a checkup. But I can't reach her. Is
the pain going to be like this all month? I'll be a crazy
lady."

"I'll call the hospital and get somebody to phone you. Are you alone?"

"No—I've just spent a quiet night here with the Detroit Lions."

"Let me reach the hospital. I'll call right back."

"Thank you. I'll be right here on the floor waiting."

Six thirty. Telephone wizard, why don't you ring? Because my connection pins are missing.

Mistresses are supposed to be glamorous creatures who go to dinner at expensive places in sexy black dresses and sit in dark corners in the flickering candlelight. Roses every morning after the night before. Brian gave me roses on Valentine's Day and Mother sent a Fanny Farmer heart.

Ringringring!

"Yes?"

"I've reached Dr. Rawji and she said she would call you as soon as she gets to the hospital in a half hour. Are you all right?"

"Uh, huh."

"Is there anybody you can call?"

"Well, I have one friend, but she worked late last night—she's a reporter."

"If you have to, call me back."

"This isn't the baby, is it?"

"Probably not."

"OK."

Six forty-five. Hot coals are shuffling around my insides. The sizzles come from the left, come from the right, stand up, sit down, fight, fight, fight! I crawl into the bathroom and sit on the toilet, allowing myself to cry softly. Needles, pins, hooks and hot coals. If only I could find the secret valve through which to release the real pain, the incredible foulness. The pain I can touch is only the beginning: A lifetime of finely executed torture I have chosen to invest upon myself is waiting at the door. Come in, anonymity. Can you read me? No. Adoption has no call letters. *Indeed, the terror of your dreams saw things to come clearly.*

I take up my pallet on the floor again next to the telephone. *Woman, be sure your heart is brave; you can take much.* This Cassandra lies wrapped in a rough wool shroud and sweats profusely and the praise rings hollow in her heart.

Did I ever think I would beat the rap of being female? I certainly didn't think within a year of leaving home I'd end up barefoot and pregnant. I always thought I knew all the numbers.

I should have known I was grooming myself for disaster. Right back when I opted to accept pain if it was necessary for my writing. How long have I been unfit for love? Passion I can understand.

I am passionately in love with Brian.

But pain is the only reality tonight. Let us groan child, let us mourn our mutual loss . . . baby, your timing is off, you are too early.

Timing.

Doesn't Brian know that the time for us is now?

I want Brian to leave wife and kids for me because God how badly I want a love with him that continues, a love that contains our child. He says he will or might leave but can't right away. "After this is over" is what he says.

Our baby will never be over.

Seven ten. Ring.

"Dr. Rawji, what is going on? The pain is a monster. I hurt like——"

"You know the baby's not due for a month. When I

saw you a few days ago, there were no signs you were anywhere near yet. Take a few aspirins and try to rest. Call me back if that doesn't work."

I've already had four aspirins. I won't take more. I will get into bed. *Et verbum caro factum est.* And dwelt among us.

If only I could still believe. Then I could put this pain into purgatory, offer it up for the poor souls. I could suck the opiate of Jesus Christ and Holy Salvation and then everything wouldn't be so futile. Genuflection and incense and worry beads we call rosaries may seem like a sham, but atheism is hell. I wish I could pray, but the rule is, You have to believe first.

Ooooohhh . . . aaahhhhhh . . . needles and pins who sticks you in? Child, I don't want to do what I am going to, but I cannot do otherwise.

The godless woman had been shaken in the night by floating terrors when she sent these offerings.

And I thought I was terrible when I stole from the dime store. I put out my hand and came up with two plastic babies, two-for-a-nickel babies. I put them in my pocket, and forgot them. Until I was going to confession a few weeks later and had on the same jacket. I was just about to go into church when I stuck my hand in my pocket and came up with New Sins! *Father forgive me for I have sinned, I stole two plastic babies from the dime store. And when I grow up I am going to GiveARealOneAway.*

The flames lick me again. What's going on? Christ Almighty . . . child of mine, while you're still inside me, still with me, are you making me suffer for what I am about to do to you?

Gin, gin, let us have some gin.

I run an ice cube over my face, on my eyes, down

my breasts, making the nipples hard: nipples never to be suckled.

Pouring the gin is difficult because I am shaking. Funny, all the clichés come true: The other woman always gets hurt, he never leaves the little wife and babies.

I collapse into a chair in the living room, the straw one from Mexico that looks better than it feels.

Eight thirteen. Sun's shining. Outside.

And I'm in here acting out a Greek soap opera.

For my morning hymns, I shall sing *mea culpas*.

God, please remember, the baby is the Holy Innocent. I am the prodigal mother. What's going on down there? My ass is burning now. My womb is a carrion of localized hell. Will aspirin and gin anesthetize?

Let us be rational. I read that a few hours before the baby is born, the water breaks, and there is a big rush of urine. I have had a terrible time controlling my bladder in the last few days. There I was talking to the lady next door, when suddenly, I felt wet and clammy on my legs and the urine was running down. I said, I have to go, and ran away with wet pants. I don't think she noticed. What's this water on my leg? Pee! This can't be the water breaking, this is only a little bit. I am so rotten I am decomposing.

It is meet and just. I no longer believe, but I still know the words.

Baby and I drink another gin-on-the-rocks. I put on a record: "That's Why I'm Drinking Again." And I change into a long flannel nightgown, the kind with little pink posies on it, the kind that nice girls and mommies wear. Me, I'm fit for a masquerade. I resume my station in the lumpy chair and listen to the words:

"We loved, we laughed, we cried, and then suddenly love died. . . ."

I must believe in Brian and me. I have no choice

tonight. He says we're rare. I'll say. I am dying and I dare not phone him.

Now the pain rushes in again, tongues of fire at my vagina, my rectum, all of my hips and stomach dissolving into a flash fire. Urine on my leg again.

Eight fifty-eight.

I phone Dr. Rawji. She again assures me I am not having the baby, but now relents and says that I should come to the hospital. I call Julie. She was still sleeping, but she will be right over.

In twenty minutes, I'm back on the floor again. My rectum is a glowing ring of fire, the mass of my stomach bursting with a thousand unseen white coals. If this is a false alarm, I'll die when I get to the real thing.

Julie. Holds me up down three flights of stairs. Car. Driving. Fast. Forsythia in bloom mock me with their yellow flash. Hospital. Wheel chair. No tears. Cheerful lady. Me on a bed. Naked. Then in a gauzy number. Lady looks at vagina. Please tell me, lady, it's all right to have official pain.

"You've already started dilating."

I will never have to go through this again.

A woman in the next bed moans loudly, she is almost screaming. Now that I have an audience, I will be silent. Sweat and tears are enough. My rectum is the size of a baseball, and the cramps that are coming now make me rise up on my elbows. I open my mouth to cry out, but no sound comes.

"I've got three children," the lady says. "When you see your baby, you'll forget all about the pain."

Father, forgive them for they know not what they do.

Dr. Rawji arrives. "I guess the aspirins wouldn't have done much." I hear the smile in her voice: Having a baby is not supposed to be so really terrible: a natural act.

My rectum is splitting up to my spine. My vagina is a throbbing wound connected to the brain's pain center. A vagina that is ripping, tearing, burning.

God help me please, let me be strong, let the baby be OK, God if you're there or if you're not—please help. Help. Oh my baby, your birth by fire is how we say good-bye.

Now I scream. For all the morning, noon and night terrors yet to come. I grip the hand of my lady and dig in my fingernails, stopping only when I see blood.

"I'm sorry." I stink, lady, but I am polite. I am a good Catholic girl.

I scream and beg for anesthesia.

If women knew, would they still have babies?

A whitewash comes with a mask over my face and I hungrily suck in, praying for numbness and oblivion. A minute later—or I don't know how long I'm gone—I'm back, the fires roasting me more than ever, hell closing in on me. Please, please, the gas, give me the gas!

It never lasts long enough.

Remember when I found out where babies came from, Mother? I was five. And remember I said I'd die if I ever had a baby, and you laughed?

I'm right.

God and Mother, I'm sorry it's turning out this way.

Happy birthday to the Fifth of April, 1966! Wheeling along to the operating room. Everything there is pea soup green. A doctor—I've never seen him before—nods with smiling eyes behind a mouth mask. The nurses do not smile. It's going to be over soon, thank you God.

Does everyone assembled here today know that I'm

unholy and unwed? The gold wedding band I wear is only to fool the public.

Fluorescent lamps give off sparkly shards, flashes of the spectrum are now dancing a dance in my eyes. Clock says: one twenty.

It was a girl.

5

Afterbirth

Everywhere the color of apricots: the fabric of the partition. The recovery room. Mrs. Hera next to my bed. A priest standing by.

The pain is over and the child is gone. And the offerings too small for the deed. *Pour out all your possessions to atone for one act of blood, you waste your work, it is all useless. . . .*

Mrs. Hera: "It's all over."

Me: "The baby—is the baby all right?"

"Yes, she's fine. You had a girl."

"A girl? What time is it?"

Just after two.

And then I yell and scream and sob and sit up and fall back down and sit up again and slam myself down against the sheets. The figures blur and colors go gray. I can't see. And then I can. I shudder and clack my teeth together and let the terror tumble out.

My baby is gone.

I am at the top of the stairs, throwing her down, down, into the unknown. And now I am the one who moans: the farewell dirge.

Tears are streaming down my face, mucus running from my nose, sweat knitting even over my toes. *I never knew how great the loss could be, even of sadness; there was a sort of joy in sorrow when he was at my side.*

I pound on the mattress; I try to throw myself on the gray marble floor. Suitable slab. Mrs. Hera holds me back.

"Let me be! Crazy!" squeaks out amid the choking, the sobbing, the gasping for air.

A nurse runs in and runs out again.

I am hysterical. This is what it is like. Let me be crazed now because now is the right time, it will never be so right again. I will contain this later, but I need this hour of madness! Does no one understand this is part of the cleansing process, this is my afterbirth?

"Lorraine, listen to me," Mrs. Hera is shouting over my screams, shaking me by the shoulders. "The baby is fine, but she weighs under five pounds because she's a premie. She's not really in danger, but as a precaution— just in case—such little babies are usually baptized. That's why the priest is here."

"Yes! Yes! Are you sure she's not going to die?" *After all the trouble kid, you've got to make it. Oh God, she's not the guilty party, take her to heaven, don't let her go to limbo. God, yes, I know, it's me. . . .*

"Are you fooling me? She's all right?"

I listened to my voice: thin, cracking in the air.

"She's in an incubator, everything is all right."

And then I start moaning all over again. Sitting up and slamming myself back down on the thin pad that passes as a mattress.

She who had been inside my body, who had been one with me, with whom I had held innumerable conversations, the baby I had tried to kill but didn't, the baby I loved, the baby who caused so much pain, this love child, my baby is now a missing person.

Good-bye my child, know that here is a mother who loves you, who will always love you and think of you, feel you there in the night when the bogeymen are out and during the day when they're not. Look, it was hard having you inside my body, and I didn't feel proud as a mother should, but at least you were mine for a while. I'm sorry it has to be this way.

You're all alone too, there in some hard plastic box with doctors and nurses—strangers—looking after you. God, please make them take good care of my child. I am deserting her and she needs you, everybody. She needs parents who live in split-level suburbia and pink booties and satin hair ribbons and bandages when she falls down and patent leather shoes and bedtime stories and help with her homework and poetry and dancing lessons and birthday parties and maybe even a white rabbit fur coat like the one I had when I was a little girl, and most of all, she needs hugs and kisses and all the love she can feel. Mine goes up into the air, and she doesn't even know of it.

The priest is still there. "Baptize her!"

"Do you have a name?"

I have no right to that.

The priest: "How is Mary?"

How terribly plain. "Yes!"

Immaculate Mary, our hearts are on fire. . . .

More raging.

The nurse is back with another nurse and a man in white. He is holding a hypodermic needle.

"Let me be crazy!"

"Now, now, this will just help to quiet you down."

I look to Mrs. Hera for help. She is holding my hand. But I know she won't stop the synthetic sanity coming my way.

I grab one of the nurses in the breast. "Gotcha!" Then I hit her in the arm. Hard. Then she comes down on my arm and pins it against the pad. Someone has the other arm. I try to pull away from the cotton swab one of the nurses is brandishing. Alcohol pricks my nose. I know they have won, but I spit at someone anyway. They have no right to lobotomize me.

The doctor is grim, I didn't feel the needle go in. I couldn't fight with my body anymore, so I lie back and let out the gut sobs I still had the strength to minister to. One of the nurses stays while I sail back into the fury of my squall.

> *Shall I call it that, or death*
> *Where is the end?*
> *Where shall the fury of fate*
> *be stilled to sleep, be done with?*

I awoke in the late afternoon in a regular hospital bed in a regular room. There were flowers on the table beside me. The card said they were from Mrs. Hera.

There was someone else in the room, in fact there were several people, three women surrounding a figure on the next bed.

Slowly, I let my fingers walk down my stomach. It was flat and soft and empty. I was sore. And I was too tired to cry.

It was over. I was still breathing, and thinking, and therefore, I had not died.

Or so it seemed.

6

Two Improper Strangers

The late-day sun filtered through the greening filigree of a tree outside the window and played on the tiled wall, pale green. This was the new wing of the hospital and all the fixings were fresh. My room was connected to another. I couldn't see the women in the other room, nor could I tell from their murmuring voices whether or not they were married.

The three women surrounding my roommate wore their dull winter coats like shrouds. One of them moved slightly, and I could see the face of the person on the bed. She looked at me and I looked back at her: She wasn't married either.

It was early evening by the time Brian got there. He brought a dozen red roses. They did not seem like enough, nothing he could do seemed like enough, that is, unless he left the wife and came to me before it was too late.

But I said nothing of the sort. I lay my head on his shoulder and let his arms enfold me, for that way, the world was almost not catching up with us. I gushed over the roses and I said it had been hard but thank you, I am fine.

Brian, there is still time for us to keep her. "How did you find out?" was what I said.

"Mrs. Hera called me at the paper around three thirty. She told me who she was and then said you had a girl and were fine." *Of course, I am fine. Women don't die when they have babies.*

"You never spoke to her before, did you?" *No reason to. This kind of birth is a rather solitary affair.*

"She asked me if I was coming to see you tonight." *Of course you would. Thank God you care that much.*

"Did you tell Owen?"

"Hm, huh. He sends his regards." For a speedy recovery, no doubt.

ACE REPORTER GIVES BIRTH
FATHER IS POLITICAL COLUMNIST

I could see the banner headline in 60-point type, thick, black letters screaming off the page. I felt like they were emblazoned on my forehead in place of a scarlet letter.

"I woke up around three last night," Brian continued, "and thought about calling you, but decided it was too late." *And so you lie in the dark, lie next to her.*

"Mrs. Hera said that your name would be on the original birth certificate, but that one goes in the sealed records," I began. "A new one is made out when she is adopted, and that's the one she uses."

"I'm glad it's on a piece of paper somewhere."

"Me too," I said lamely.

"But it won't be in the birth announcements in the newspapers."

We both managed a wry grin.

"Darlin', I love you."

I know you do, but could you please do something about it? And quickly? The time for merely words is slipping by. The party is over.

He stayed for well over an hour and then he was gone, not back to our funny apartment with the burlap I'd put on the walls and the tea cart I had refinished and the small round table where we ate, but to his home in the suburbs, a big red brick house with white wooden shutters and a yard out back where his other kids played. When I took the chance, I used to drive by. One time I saw his daughter outside. I stepped on the gas and flew around the corner.

I spent a long time arranging the roses. Now I had two bouquets. Like valentines.

My roommate turned out to be a chubby teen-ager with acne and overbleached hair the color of white sand. She was "almost sixteen."

"Are you, ah, connected with Southlawn Terrace?"

She simply nodded.

There was a slight pause as we let that sink in.

"But my boyfriend and I, we want to get married," she started breathlessly. "We tried to elope, but his mother stopped us. Drove down to Maryland, but she sent the police after us and they found us before we could get married."

Is this girl out of her mind? Married at fifteen? She should be thinking about what to wear to the junior prom. A few months ago, I would have called her stupid.

"You're going to give the baby away, aren't you?"

Please join me in this act of terror.

"I don't know. I had a boy, and Ronnie wants me to keep him, even if we can't get married right now. We can later, and we'll have our own son. My mother said I could bring the baby home and live there. I would drop out of school and get a job at Dunkin' Donuts, or something."

There goes your life.

"Could you give the child all the things he needs? Aren't you too young to take on such a heavy responsibility?"

"That's what I hear from the social worker, more or less. And Ronnie's mother."

"I think they're right."

"My mother doesn't want me to. Says I'll be sorry."

The kid has a better chance being adopted, he'll get two parents, two grown-ups who can afford him, physically and emotionally. I imagine it will be a zoo if you take him home.

So what?

"I don't know. I was thinking I could work during the day and finish school at night. Or not finish school. Don't like it much."

There wasn't anything I could say that made any sense, really.

"Are you going to see your baby?" she wanted to know.

"I don't think I can stand it." A face to remember all my life, a face on that baby in that dream. "She's a premie, and so they can't bring her to me anyway." Thank God for small favors.

"I'm going to walk down to the nursery tomorrow with my mother."

And I'll lie here like a stone.

My stomach is flat. And baby is gone. Now there is just me again.

There was a full-length mirror on the bathroom door, and I stood there, mother of two days, for a long time, looking at my stomach which was now so empty. It had been years since I was so thin. I had watched my weight during the pregnancy and gained only a few pounds; but I had been a little overweight to begin, and so she took the weight from the rest of me. My face was spare, my thighs were slim, my wrists, which had always been no larger than a child's, now seemed fragile enough to crack.

The last thing you look like is an earth mother. You are fashionably slim now. Isn't that wonderful? Your old clothes will have to be taken in.

They call me: biological mother. I hate those words. They make me sound like a baby machine, a conduit, without emotions, as if this thing just happened and now it is over and they are going to tell me that I must put it behind me and go out and make a new life. One, two, three, just like that. But I must not allow myself pity, or I will crack.

I have a baby.

Go see her.

I can't.

She wants to look at you.

She'll never know the difference.

Are they taking good care of her in this place? Is she doing all right?

I wonder how much I weigh.

Selfish slut, all you care about is yourself. See the thin lady, isn't she pretty? Does she look a little crazy, there around the eyes, I think I see something suspicious.

I wish I could go home and tell them.

They don't need the extra pain. You can handle this yourself. And why don't I admit it? I am too proud to do otherwise.

That's part of the reason you're not home on their doorstep. It had been difficult to leave and it would have been a lot harder to go back and admit defeat in front of them and the neighbors and all those carefully Catholic cousins. Coming home pregnant at twenty-three certainly couldn't count as being able to manage one's life well. They'll never have to know. What would be the point?

At the end of the eighth grade, you signed up for the courses you would take in the ninth. Girls took shorthand and typing, unless you were going to college; then you took algebra and Latin.

I filled in the form and calmly presented it to my father for his signature. He was sitting at the kitchen table reading the newspaper.

"What's this?" he asked.

"My classes for next year."

"Latin? What good is that going to do you?" I could hear the undertone of a sneer, but I kept on going.

"I need it for college. St. Al's doesn't have any other languages, and you need two years to get into college."

"COLLEGE!! You're not going to any college—you're going to end up getting married and having kids, just like everybody else. You can work as a secretary until then. I know you're smart, sometimes too smart for your own good. Anyway, college is a waste of time for girls."

Who is this man? Who does he think he is? Who does he think he is talking to? This is me.

We know I am a girl, but that's never stopped us before. That didn't stop you when you came to my room at night and told me stories about your high jinks in that poor coal mining town you grew up in. And remember the stories you made up about little girls who flew airplanes and went on safaris in Africa and sailed down the Amazon and got in and out of boiling pots of oil? I know, when you were thirteen you had to drop out of school and become a coal miner like your father, and now I am thirteen and I tell you, I am going to college. This is 1956 and you have a good job working for a construction company and I can so go to college.

And maybe I'll get married and maybe I won't, and maybe I'll have children and maybe I won't.

"I am going to go to college." Do not get hysterical. He's the crazy one, it says so here in my head. "I do not want to be a secretary." I will die first. "I want to be a newspaper reporter."

"Lorraine, you'll go to college and you'll meet somebody and that will be the end of that. We don't have that kind of money to throw around." So you think you can throw away my future?

"I'll put myself through school."

"You don't know what you are talking about. Who even put that idea in your head?"

"Nobody." For starters you, you silly goat. Remember when you took me flying on my fifth birthday and I got to sit next to the pilot? I will fly a plane someday too.

"Lorraine, be reasonable. . . ."

It's you who aren't. You even know I can do it. How can you be doing this to me, Harry? You're my special father, and I'm your special daughter, your only daughter, and we've always been close and I always thought you knew this thing, that I would go to college, and grow up and do something, just like a man.

"Look," he continued, "I don't want to hurt your feelings, but we're not some ritzy family that can send its girls to college. It would be a waste."

This girl is going. My grandfather—you told me—was a palace guard for the czar and came to this country by himself. And my grandmother was raised in a big house with servants and music teachers and fancy dress balls, and she left it behind in the old country and came over here all by herself and got a job playing a concertina in a restaurant in Boston, and you think any grandchild of those two people can't go to college? Think again. I was fighting back the tears and staring at the grain in the oak table-top as if it were the dorm plan of the University of Michigan.

Father rattled his newspaper.

"Just because George went to college doesn't mean you can. His family has money. And besides, he's a *man*."

I can't help the fact that I am a girl. George was like a brother, and he had been a part of the family for as long as I could remember. His parents owned a bowling alley and because that kept them busy, George came over to our house almost every day at least once. He could walk in without ringing the doorbell and he could argue with my father and he could go upstairs and read in my brother's room and play the stereo whether or not Richard was home. When George was in college, he liked the banana story so much he took it to his teachers at the University of Detroit and they guessed I was a few years older than I was and the paper ended up being used as an example of something or other in one of George's courses. George was a school teacher now and we knew I should go to college.

"George didn't put this idea in my head." Spoken barely above a whisper. I was still fighting off the tears. It wasn't his words that bothered me so much—I knew that somehow I would get a college degree—but what they meant: The special empathy I thought my father and I had was going up in smoke and we would never quite be the same after that. Maybe that was the day I grew up, the first time I figured that no man was ever going to look out for me, that who I was and what I did would be my signature to the world, and that it was important to do something, because being only some man's wife and some child's mother and nothing else would never be enough. I had trusted Harry, and now look where it got me.

Mother walked into the room. She had been watching television in the living room.

"What's going on? You two look as if you just lost your best friend."

Right.

"Lorraine wants to take *Latin* next year. For *college.*"

"Oh? Well?"

"*Well,* it's ridiculous. In the first place, she's a girl."

Even she didn't answer that.

Mother was like all the other women of Dearborn, that suburb of Dertoit where the garbage collections are terrific and the city wins awards for being the cleanest in the U.S.A. and the pansy is the official flower. Mother made tomato soup cake and mashed potatoes and gravy the way Harry liked them and the best butter frosting in town, even though she never quite believed it was.

What was surprising about Mother not agreeing right off with Harry was that she was the one I had the fights with about reading when she thought I should be outside playing with the other kids on the block or at least helping her get dinner; she was the one who was always after me at night to put down the book, shut out the light, and get to sleep. Mother and I, we always fought because I wasn't turning out at all like her sister's kids and I gave no indication that I was about to change. My cousins never talked about careers the way I did, and I had told my mother I would die if I ever had a child. Don't know why, it just popped into my head.

I have been born into the wrong family. That's it. There is some mistake.

"You have to sign it." Or I will forge your signature.

"I don't have to sign anything." He went back to his newspaper.

Mother stayed out of this battle. Mostly, my father and I stopped talking to one another. Suppers, which had always been noisy affairs during which we'd talk about what happened at work and what I was studying in school or about my collection of Lincoln pennies or things we read in the newspaper, now became dreary silences my mother filled as best she could, being overly pleasant and asking a lot of questions that didn't need answers. But I couldn't go to her for help because I didn't see how she could, not really. After all, if I did not go to college, she would undoubtedly end up with the kind of daughter she thought she wanted, one who married a nice boy and settled down nearby and had grandchildren. What was surprising is that as far as I knew, she said nothing to Harry about college one way or the other and when we talked about it, she seemed to be on my side. So what if I was a girl? Didn't I make the honor roll?

But if she never told me I had to give in, she didn't argue my case. Or at least, I don't think so. Harry was a hard man to oppose, once he made up his mind. Then again, I was his daughter.

A week or two passed. The day to turn in the registration forms came and went. I made excuses to the nun.

I heard my father and George talking loudly about Lorraine and college once. I didn't go downstairs, but listened from the stairway. That was my whole life they were talking about. George kept saying that she's got the brains, she could make something of herself, there were scholarships, it could be done.

One morning I came down to breakfast before anyone but my father was there, sipping coffee and reading *The Free Press,* the way he did every morning. I put the slip in front of him and said, "You going to sign this, or not?"

He scrawled his name on the bottom line.

"Now this doesn't mean anything, you know?"

Someday you'll be proud, Daddy.

That summer I turned fourteen, Harry took the family to Beaver Island, and the breach between us healed, more or less. We were beginning to go our separate ways, never as simple as it sounds. Don't quite know why we make such a fuss over it, but we do. Parents don't want to let go, and their children know they must, and until it all gets down, there's a mess of confusion and grumbling that goes on, and when it's over, it's all quite a relief.

Anyway, Beaver Island. It was the kind of place my father and I felt right at home in, with a weird past and an uncertain future and a story around every corner. Good fishing, too. You couldn't exactly call Beaver Island a ghost town, because somewhat less than two hundred people lived there year round back then, close to a quarter of a century ago. Once it had been an honest-to-God Mormon kingdom. A splinter group had broken off from the sect on its way west and took up residence there, thirty-two miles out in the center of Lake Michigan. I guess they figured the Indians already there wouldn't bother them, and neither would mainlanders, only that's not what happened. The people back in Charlevoix, which is from where the ferry still comes and goes, didn't take to the Mormons' seemingly wanton ways one bit, especially after King James Strang killed a man and none of the witnesses would testify at the trial. And after Strang was shot by a group of his unhappy followers, the mainlanders said enough is enough, and a few battles ensued between them and the Mormons. If you go to Charlevoix, you can find a monument to the folks who died. But I'm getting off the track, sort of.

One day the mainlanders arrived in force and told the Mormons they had to clear out, just like that, on the next passing ship. Thing was, the *Northern Star* was due in four hours. And so that was the end of the Mormons on Beaver Island.

After that there was a whole group of Irish immigrants who set up a commercial fishing industry there, and maybe a couple of thousand people lived on Beaver Island in the early nineteenth century. But then the lamprey eel came swimming down the St. Lawrence Seaway, killed a lot of the fish, and the Irish left. We kept hearing how terrible the fishing was, but Harry and I decided to try it anyhow, just because the lake was there and a rowboat came with our cottage. Best fishing we ever had.

Drive around the island and you find the remnants of the Mormon farmhouses: silver boards dully glistening in the sand. Some still stood back then. A pack of wild horses, descendants of those set free by the Mormons, roamed the island.

A map showed a town other than St. James, so we drove by where Nomad was supposed to be, and didn't see anything other than trees and fields and bushes that

looked like they had been there a long time. We kept
thinking we must have missed the town, so we drove back
and forth a few times. It wasn't there anymore.

The law on Beaver Island was a one-armed game
warden, which delighted my father no end because that
just made the place more peculiar, and the screwier something was, the more my father warmed up to it. The game
warden's duties were never made clear, but they did not
include telling the Indians who still lived there that they
should change the license plates on their old pickup trucks
annually.

St. James consisted of three bars, the King Strang
Hotel, two general stores—each with a gasoline pump—a
restaurant, a post office, a Catholic church and a Baptist
church, and the ramshackle offices and printing plant of a
newspaper that was no more. Heard they made that into a
museum. Nuns taught at the public school because regular
teachers wouldn't stay. There was a doctor the first summer
we were there, but then he retired and went to live on the
mainland, and although money had come from somewhere
to build a small modern clinic, Beaver Island couldn't
keep a doctor much more than a year or two. Eventually,
the old doctor moved back. Don't know what's happening
now.

Beaver Island is seven miles wide and fourteen miles
long, depending on where you measure. If you're out walking in the woods, the thing to do is take a big stick along
to try to ward off the many snakes that are likely to cross
your path. Not all of them are harmless. Beaver Island
is sometimes called Emerald Island, and I used to think
that when St. Patrick got the snakes to leave the other one,
they were all miraculously transferred to Beaver Island.

Harry and I spent hours talking to the folks at the
general stores, ferreting out all we could about the place,

and we roamed around more than a bit. Mother usually stayed close to the cottage, crocheting edges for pillow slips and baking cakes, and taking care of my brother Tom, who was only three.

One time Harry and I decided to shove out into the water with the old raft that we found down the bay a ways from our place. We also came upon some long poles, maybe twelve feet long or more—don't know what they might have been for—and off we went. We didn't really go anywhere, we went out thirty feet or thereabouts, and came back and drifted around the shore, daring the water to get deeper than the poles were long, because when that happened we were out of control, and that's when the fun began. The water was a mite choppy and slopping up on the raft, and the day looked as if it was hankering for a rain storm, and although we said nothing, we were aware that lots of people had died in Lake Michigan when they didn't think they were going to, and the more chancy the situation became, the more that raft became our *Kon-Tiki*.

Harry never made me feel that because I was a girl I wasn't supposed to run fast and be strong and get cold and wet when the occasion demanded. And when mother complained how inept I was in the womanly arts, neither Harry nor I paid much attention. Somehow I figured I would never need to know, or I would learn on the spot.

Wandering around by myself on Beaver Island, I discovered a shack at the end of a long, rickety dock. I peered through the single window: A man inside was sitting at a plain wooden table and pecking away at a typewriter. A bare light bulb hung overhead. I knocked on the door. He and I talked for a few moments and I don't recall much of the specifics except that was a retired professor from Michigan State University and he was writing a book and his wife was with him on the island. I said, I am going to be a writer and I already am one, sort of, and besides that, I keep a diary. He told me to keep on writing, that's what makes writers, and said why didn't I come back to visit again. I was elated.

But when I ran home and told Harry about the great thing that had just happened, it got changed into something altogether different. Harry didn't actually say the man might be a child molester, but that's how it came out. Mother explained it to me when I couldn't understand why Harry got so upset and said I could not go back. Of course I meant to, even if I got found out, but somehow I didn't have a chance before we left the island. I never knew his name. He probably doesn't remember our meeting in the shack, people are always remembering different things.

I think Harry was only trying to keep me from being hurt if it turned out that I didn't realize my dreams. Of course, I don't know what he wanted to be when he was a kid growing up poor in a coal mining town, but I do know that he wanted to go to South America when I knew him. But by then he had a family to take care of. He was the foreman of a construction company and got to drive around in a red pickup truck. A Ford. He had had to quit school when he was thirteen, and go down in the mines; and by the time he was seventeen, he was a gang boss like his father, who died that year. And so my father became the head of a household of seven. He was the square dance caller in town too.

He used to sing to me at night in his flat, nasal twang, sing the songs of Jenners, Pennsylvania, such as "May I Sleep in Your Barn Tonight, Mister?" (for it's cold lying on the ground), which went to the tune of "Red River Valley." Guess I still know almost all the words.

You couldn't actually call Harry handsome. He was slim and sinewy, just under six feet tall. He was finely chiseled everywhere, and his angular patrician nose fit just fine on his face. His skin was sallow and deeply etched with laugh lines and he wore his dark thin hair combed straight back because he wouldn't be bothered with a lot of things like that, such as which tie went with his Sunday suit. He just didn't give a damn about what people thought; he was true to himself. He was awful at small talk, and at weddings, christenings, and other such "gala affairs"— which is what he called them—he'd lapse into silence, find some corner and sit and wait until he could reasonably suggest it was time to go. My mother, usually lively, often a downright belle, complained that Harry didn't know how to enjoy himself. He'd look at me and I'd look back at him: We knew we knew how to enjoy. His eyes, the color of rust, were the kind that can read your mind. Scratch him, and you'd strike tempered steel.

Sometimes I called him Harry; sometimes I called him Dad. But what I remember about calling him Harry is that it made me feel that we weren't just like every other father and daughter. We were a whole lot closer, practically plugged into one another's thoughts, we were friends and equals. And so when he said I couldn't go visit the writer, or that I couldn't go to college, it was much too late to undo what he had already given me: the belief that I could do with my life anything I'd set my mind to.

In my junior year of high school, I had a job after school as a soda jerk, I wrote a column for the weekly newspaper in Dearborn, and I became editor in chief of the high school newspaper.

"YOU ARE CRAZY TO SPEND SO MUCH TIME

ON THAT STUPID PAPER!" my mother explained. "That damn paper—it takes up all your time and you never get paid a cent! What good is it ever going to do you? What are you possibly learning that you can use in your life later on? Or that column! Every Tuesday you're up until midnight and then you have to drive to east Dearborn to drop it off! For what? They could pay you! You're not some movie star's daughter! You better get that idea right out of your head now or you're going to be sorry. You're just going to get hurt. You are going to fix dinner for us on Sunday, you could learn more from helping around the house!"

"Mother, I can't fix dinner on Sunday," I began, grimly, through my teeth. "There's a special meeting of the editors of the *Excalibur*."

"That paper—you even get a pimple every month when it's due!"

"It's my period."

"Ha!"

I know I am not some movie star's daughter, but I am going to be a writer, no matter what it takes, and anyway, I already am one.

And as soon as I can, I am going to leave this town. Don't fit here, never did.

I entered Wayne State University in downtown Detroit. By my junior year, I was paying for my education (so that I could become a newspaper reporter on a big city daily) by working as a reporter for *The Dearborn Guide*, the weekly that took my columns when I was sixteen. That, plus a stipend from the university for being an editor of the college daily, paid for my tuition, my carfare and my lunches. My father only rarely mentioned anymore that I should become a nurse or a teacher so that I could fit my work schedule around the children he knew I would end up having.

In my junior year, I ran for editor in chief of *The Daily Collegian*. There had not been a woman editor since the Korean War, at least, and now it was the early sixties. Another woman on the staff convinced me to run, and even though at the onset, I knew I didn't have much of a chance, by the time I had written a précis on how I would run the paper, lined up my top editors, and sat through an interview with a student-faculty committee, I wanted that job. By that time, I wouldn't admit even to myself that my chances were about as good as those of a southern Republican running for office during Reconstruction a century earlier.

My competition was not only tall, male and handsome, he had a story of triumph over near-death going for him. In Ray's sophomore year, he had a cerebral hemorrhage. At first we heard he might die. Then we heard he would never get out of bed again. Then we heard he would never get out of a wheelchair. Then we heard if he walked, it would always be on crutches. And then he came back to school, a year later, wearing a leg brace that was mostly hidden by his pants. He walked with a slight limp. He had been popular with the women before, but now they absolutely melted like cherry Popsicles in August. To be his girl was to be envied: Not only could you mother him, you could, well, he was sexy. Like a movie star. He had a wry sense of humor shot through with cynicism, but the next minute he was sweet, tender, blue eyes sincere as all get out. He knew exactly what he was doing. I am sure that he has inspired more fantasies than any other man I've ever met.

Naturally, he won. The night I learned that he won, I

wept and phoned my mother. When I dried my tears, I vowed that I would succeed, I wouldn't get beaten down by the system, even though I knew I had been born the wrong sex. I would prove to everybody and myself that I had what it takes.

He chose a man to be managing editor and asked me to stay on as copy editor, third in command. It was the job I'd held the year before.

Now the guys who entered the race and lost always quit the *Collegian,* who needs it anyway, and got a job with one of the downtown dailies and rarely came around the newspaper office anymore after that. But I was a woman, I had to do more to stay even. Besides, I didn't think I could get a job downtown, even though I had sold them a story or two, and I wanted to keep the weekly column I wrote and I liked the camaraderie, so I stayed on. The *Collegian* was my social life, since I hadn't joined a sorority or much else. When was there time? And I had felt for years that the kind of people who gravitated to newspapering were the most interesting around. Hard boiled? That's just a cover, underneath they're all suckers for another hard-luck story.

The managing editor Ray chose proved to be more concerned about being a nice guy and not hurting anybody's feelings and running a pizza business on the side than managing a daily newspaper. He was fired before Thanksgiving. Ray asked me if I would take over. Ray also asked me to a screening of *Dr. Strangelove.* I accepted both.

In the spring of 1964, the Ford Motor Company introduced the Mustang. That may be of only passing interest to you, but to the editors of the thirty largest college dailies in the country, it meant that they got to drive around a red convertible free for a month before graduation. Part of the promotion to introduce the Mustang.

In 1964, I got to sit in the passenger's seat and change the cassettes in the tape deck.

I never even asked if I could drive the red Mustang because that would have been asking for a special privilege, and dammit, I felt like I deserved it. Except for that accident of biology. I was being denied what I wanted because my genitals were different. There were times when I questioned if my desire to succeed somehow wasn't unfitting and unfeminine; such introspection usually was prodded by someone I was dating who would just drop the barest of hints that maybe I was not normal. It at least made me pause.

Graduation approached and the interviews for jobs began: Are you going to get married? Do you have a steady boyfriend? Are you planning on having children? Yes, they actually asked those questions.

I swear, you can trust me, I am not going to quit. Yes, I have a boyfriend, but we're not planning to get married right now and even if we did, it wouldn't mean anything in terms of my career. You see, just like a man, I am going to fit my personal life around my professional.

When I told my family I had accepted a job on *The Saginaw News,* ninety miles from home, I might as well have announced that I was taking up residence in a brothel.

"Nice girls don't leave home until they get married! You should stay here! Why do you want a place of your own unless you want to . . . be with men. None of your cousins have such crazy ideas and what makes you think you're so special? You don't seem like my daughter. Where did you get these crazy ideas? Lorraine, you're going to be sorry one day, everything for a career, and then what are you going to have? I'll tell you—*nothing!*"

My mother had some very definite opinions about the way I was running my life.

Technically, I was still a virgin, and technically, I wanted to stay that way until I got married. Although I wanted to be a man in the work world, I did not mind adhering to the double standard sexually. Men couldn't get pregnant, could they?

My only serious romance during college had stumbled into a quagmire by the time graduation came. John and I saw each other only now and then, for he still lived in one town and I in another, and although we talked about marriage someday, that would naturally be later and after he finished college, and anyway I didn't have to think about it right now. I hoped that somehow we would be able to work it out because I believed that he wouldn't try to stop me from following my dream, he would help make it happen. But first, he had to get his college degree and we would have to find the right city for both of us. All of which would take some time, and in the meantime, I would start working as hard as I knew how. I would take the job in Saginaw, even though it was in the women's department, which is not what I had hoped. I didn't want to spend my time writing up brides, but I had no choice. I figured I could write features for the news pages as soon as I got the feel of the place.

In the meantime, my mother was dying over the fact that her only daughter was leaving home to move to a dinky apartment by herself . . . for a job? She was losing face in front of her relatives, and besides that, who knows what could happen? She stopped talking to me, except to answer yes or no. My father said that he would help me move to Saginaw when the time came.

But a few weeks before I was actually to leave, my mother woke up one morning and said, OK, what do you need to set up an apartment? What can I give you? I have two of lots of things. We went through the house and I ended up with the kinds of essentials most girls get when they have a wedding shower. It was her way of saying, look, I still don't like what you are doing, but since nothing I can do will change your mind, I might as well be your friend and give you all the help I can.

And so my parents did not know I was pregnant. I wrote them letters full of things I made up.

I was healing quickly. My body knew that this birth was an earthquake, not the measured changing of the seasons. The shudder had been released, and now my body was going back to normal as quickly as possible. The orifices that had been torn were mending rapidly. The nurses commented on it. I added up the calories on my plate and when one of the nurses discovered what I was doing, she said how terrific it was that I was getting back into shape, not like some other women.

I have to get on with my life. I do not have the luxury of looking like a mother. I don't even have any stretch marks. I started doing a few easy exercises on the bed, special postpartum ones I learned from a book. My roommate ate bonbons and thought I was slightly crazy.

Don't you see? My motherhood is almost over. I never allowed myself to get as big as a house, I hid the swelling under a sweat shirt. I don't think my landlord even knew, and he changed a light bulb for me the day before the baby was born.

I ventured to talk with the other women sharing my suite. These were married, these were delighted to be mothers. Because Brian showed up every night, and because I wore his ring on my finger, I think they assumed that I was also married. I listened to them, and I said very little. They wanted to talk about layettes and I was simply trying to make the center hold.

When the babies were on the floor, I would walk down the hall to the sitting room, which was always deserted, and for those few days, always flushed with sunlight. The room was more of a porch than a parlor and had windows on three sides from which I could see the new life of spring. Patches of green now blotted the dull winter earth; forsythia bushes punctuated the grounds like giant lemon drops. This was Holy Week.

I read magazines in the sun-room while I waited for Mrs. Hera to come. She came every day, and she brought me news of the baby. Now she no longer needed oxygen to help her breathe, she had lost a few precious ounces, but now her weight had stabilized. Now she was gaining again. But she was still in the incubator. Cold hard plastic incubator with no one to cuddle her, no one to hold her to a breast.

The breasts were bad.

Great giant orbs—no, that's a poetic fantasy, for even then I did not have more than a handful. But they were fuller than they had ever been before.

My body does not know it does not need to act like a normal woman's. The baby's not for keeping. Funny, some women who want to breast-feed can't, and others who don't want to are brimming over with milk. Funny.

My breasts ached. Left stains in my bra. I pushed my nose into the fabric and inhaled the faint sourness. Intima-

tions of what's inside. Thought you could betray your sex?
Now see what you did.

On the third day, Lydia's boyfriend came to see her.
He looked like a pimply fifteen-year-old who had unex-
pectedly been called upon to join the major leagues and
now was bewildered by what was happening around him.
He bent over so that his face was close to Lydia's, and
they whispered low so that I couldn't hear in my bed a few
feet away. I went for a walk. I always walked the opposite
direction from the nursery.

I usually ended up on the porch. I watched the sun
go down and waited for Brian. One night the sky had that
orange sherbet glow that sometimes surprises you when
the air is full of winter. The orange thinned high in the
sky to a hazy gray that shaded into cobalt blue. The room
was chilly now, and I shivered under my robe.

Brian came then.

What Brian and I did not do in those days was talk
about what we would do when this was over. Yes, I was his
woman, I heard that again and again, but no, he couldn't
leave the wife and children just yet. Please wait.

Someday Someday Someday. Really? Does he really
mean it? And why not now, this is the time I need him.

I want him so badly, but I will not beg or cry or
even look stricken, even though it kills me every minute he
continues to stay with her. He must leave because he wants
to, and come to me of his own volition. What would I gain
if by weepy gales of protestations, I made him choose? A
man who did not come to me freely. That will not suffice.
I would not feel loved enough, I would always be worried
that he did something he did not want to do, that he would
resent me eventually, and the guilt would overtake us like
wild ponies racing in the night. My guilt because I forced

him to act when he wasn't ready. His guilt because he had
left a wife and children. I will not beg. Or even talk about
us, even though I hardly think of anything else.

But the time for Brian and me is slipping away. If he
is not strong enough now, when I need him the most, will
he be tomorrow? And if he is, will that be enough?

You see, the child will be gone. Ah, yes, the child
will have been sacrificed to his procrastination. What anybody thinks about the fact that I show up at home with
a girl child is immaterial.

"Lorraine, it's time for me to go now. . . ."

Ten seconds of silence. I squeezed his hand.

"I love you," he whispered.

But not enough.

"I love you, Brian."

I cannot think about whether he will or will not leave
Kathleen and come to me. I cannot discern the answer, and
for now I need to live in illusion. I simply need to get
through the night.

On the fifth day, Saturday, it was time for me to go
home. Brian was to pick me up in the morning. I wanted to
get out of there, away from all those married ladies who
had children they got to keep. But I was leaving a child
behind.

They say even though you are small and still need an
incubator, they say you are doing fine and there is no longer
any danger you will die. I know you are going to live. I
knew it the first time you kicked me. Now my stomach
is quiet. And you are not in my arms.

I was dressed and ready to go. Brian came. I said
good-bye to Lydia and said that I hoped that everything
worked out for the best, whatever that was. She nodded
and said she would probably give the child up for adoption,

like me. We hugged one another. Brian stood there, shuffling his feet. "He loves you," Lydia whispered into my ear. "He loves you, remember that."

The teen-age volunteer in her candy-stripe pinafore came with a wheelchair. Do not break down in front of all these people. It would be stupid.

Brian went on ahead to bring the car around to the back door. I got into the wheelchair and got out again because I thought I was going to be sick. I went into the bathroom and kneeled in front of the toilet. I did not vomit.

I got back into the chair and was pushed out the door. "Good-bye, Lydia."

The wheelchair rolled smoothly down beige antiseptic halls, past hospital rooms and nursing stations and elevators and carts with the lunch meal stacked high. We did not go past the nursery.

This is the longest roller coaster ride of my life. Baby, good-bye, I am leaving you here. I am sorry. Please forgive me. Have a good life. Everybody says this is what I must do, but no, I am not at all sure it is the best. How do I know you'll get good parents? How do I know the people at the agency, even Mrs. Hera, know what they are talking about? Do not break down. Keep looking forward.

How many more corridors, how many more turns, where is the end?

Mrs. Hera told me there was a couple already picked out for you. She doesn't interview them, somebody else does. When a baby is born they have a meeting and decide who is the best couple for this particular baby. Brian and me, Brian and me. I know it.

No. We're not. We're not even an official couple.

But who are they?

The sun was shining outside.

Brian's pale blue Chevy appeared. Be a robot. Stand.

Ambulate. "Thank you." It is important to be polite. It is not her fault. She simply happens to be the one whose job it was to take me to the door. It could have been anyone. She smiled.

Brian was out of the car now. When I caught his eyes, my face shifted into a grimace, the knees felt like jelly, tears were at the rim of my eyes.

"Don't," he said, "please don't." I obeyed.

He held open the door on the passenger side and I slid in. I listened to the crunch of the gravel while we drove away. What a loud noise it made.

The next day was Easter Sunday. I telephoned my parents long-distance. I did not see Brian.

7

The Deal

"What kind of people are adopting my little girl?"

"Professional people."

"What does that mean?"

"The father could be a doctor or a lawyer, the mother a nurse or a teacher."

How incredibly dull. My daughter is going to be difficult for them to understand. She is going to be an artist of some sort. Or at least a renegade. And she needs parents who are the same. But maybe these people will have books and music and poetry and laughter . . . all lawyers and doctors and nurses and teachers are not dull.

"Which ones?"

"I can't say."

"Why not—they know a lot about me? Remember all those forms I filled out? About my grandparents and his grandparents and illness in the family and education? What about them?"

"Lorraine, we have gone over this. *It is best this way.* You will go on and although it doesn't seem possible now, you will make a new life for yourself. You will never forget your child, but the pain will become less and less with time. You must try to put this in the back of your mind."

Oh, sure.

"Time heals all wounds."

Not this one.

"Will I ever be able to find out what happened? What if she needs me? What if she wants to know me? Will I ever———"

"No, once you sign these papers, it's over. We have a nice Catholic couple for your child. You must convince yourself of that. You cannot change your mind. It would be bad for everybody. Think of the parents. Think of her."

Yes. But why can't she be able to find me someday? I will always leave a forwarding address in our file.

"What if I change my mind? Do women ever do that? Go to court and get their babies back, or find out———"

"Do not sign unless you are absolutely convinced you will not do that. You wouldn't win in court, and . . ." She shook her head.

"So there is no way she can ever find out who I am?"

Why? Why is this the best? Am I going to be reduced to looking at pictures of children in photographs, pictures in magazines, faces in newspapers, engagement and wedding pictures? And all my life?

"No. It's best this way."

And I have no right to say otherwise.

"Where is she?"

"In the nursery here. We had her checked by our doctor and she's in fine health. Well. Here are the papers."

A death warrant. Whose?

I used my own pen.

I later learned that Lydia kept her baby. Changed her mind at the last minute and took him home. Right up until the end the folks at the agency thought she was going to sign him away. But the day came, and she and Ronnie showed up together and went to the nursery to see their child one last time, and changed their mind. I never found out whether Lydia married Ronnie, but that's not really the point.

I remember that at the time, I thought Lydia had done the wrong thing for her baby, for herself. Mrs. Hera agreed. I am not sure now.

Once in a while somebody asks me what I would say to a young woman going through what I went through. Would I tell her to keep the baby at all costs?

I would tell her that if it had to be that way, if there wasn't a man to marry her, if she couldn't support herself and the child financially and emotionally, if she couldn't go the road alone, in other words, if the child had to be adopted, I would tell her to insist on meeting those parents. She is giving them her child, and she has every right in the world to meet the people who will raise her child, and yes, pass judgment and decide for herself if they are good enough. She can demand this no matter what the laws on the books say, no matter what she has been led to believe by people who have never given away a child. There is wisdom the heart knows beyond reason, where logic follows if we let it. And if the experts at the agency say you can't do it that way, I would say, too bad; I will find parents to adopt my child another way. I know it can be done.

In court I once heard a psychologist, a man who has four adopted children, explain to a judge why revealing the truth and opening the sealed records was the best way. The judge asked, but wouldn't it cause more pain than keeping the status quo?

"Adoption," the man replied, "adoption is always painful."

8

Back on the Road Again

"I see you haven't been working for a few months. What is that all about?"

Oh my God, I knew this would happen.

The city editor of the Toronto *Star* was waiting for an answer.

"My father was sick, and I went home to take care of him, to be with him." He doesn't believe me, because if that were the case and I were any good, my old paper would have taken me back. This man thinks I'm an alcoholic or he thinks I had a nervous breakdown. Hospitalized. Remember Sallie from *The Dearborn Guide?* She had a job with one of the downtown Detroit papers, and then lost it because of pills and booze. She would dry out at Northville every few years. But her career was finished. This guy thinks I was in a crazy hospital. Or that I am flaky about my work. Can he see how nervous I am, the sweat on my forehead, the pounding inside?

The city editor was a solid mass of man with a balding pate. His piercing eyes were shards of glass as they stared from my résumé to me.

I can't help it, I haven't been working for six months because I am a woman. You wouldn't know about that. You would say *how stupid can she get?* I can't tell you the truth, what would be the future in that? I am not going to get this job, I want to get out of here. There is no air.

"Why would you want to move to Toronto?"

"Why not? I like the paper . . . I like its style."

Stop playing with me.

Earlier, I had met with the managing editor who had said my stories were good. Thank you, I said, and the interview went along just fine. He did not ask what I had been doing for the last six months. I brought it up and said my father had been quite ill, heart and all that. He suggested that the city editor talk to me. He had made me think that finding a job wasn't going to be so terrible after all.

I drove eighty miles an hour and was home before dark. Brian came over and listened. He said, as he had been saying for months, that one day we would be together, that he just couldn't do it now and would I please hold on. One day, he would come for me.

I found a job as a receptionist while I scouted around for an opening on a newspaper. I wrote a lot of letters and I got a lot of rejections. Newspapers were folding like chairs in New York City, and the reporters spread out in the East created a glut on the market for a few years. I did get one or two offers, but they would have put me back in the women's department. The letters would begin, "We have no openings in the city room, but you write well and we have passed your letter and résumé on to the women's editor. . . ." Would you suggest to a young man wanting to cover government that he start with basketball? I wanted to write in reply, but I didn't because it would have been uppity and would have served no purpose I could fathom. I simply looked elsewhere. It had been a lucky break when I got out of the women's department once, and I felt the chance would never come again if I caved in to the way things were.

In the meantime, I went to a personnel agency for a temporary job. I had always made sure my typing was abysmal enough to keep me from landing a secretarial job, and it didn't fail me now. It was suggested that I could get a job as a proofreader for the other paper. No thank you, I would rather learn how to operate a switchboard.

My office was closer than comfortable to the newspaper, so I usually ate lunch at my desk. If I went for a walk, it was in the opposite direction, and I did not go downtown shopping. Brian and I never went to the old restaurants. Too risky. Once in a while, I would see the wife of a reporter at a shopping center on the outside of town, and I would dash madly in the opposite direction. I certainly didn't want to be asked: How have you been? Better to have everyone think that I cleared out because the affair with Brian got too hot to handle, if they thought about me at all.

The man I worked for said there was something strange about me working as a receptionist for a firm that sold office furniture. "You're hiding something." I smiled and said nothing. "You're much too smart for this." I agreed. "Are you an actress? You take these days off now and then and give no explanation." I nodded. Usually the type who has to tell three people something before it is real, I had suddenly become a woman of mystery.

Julie suggested that we meet for a drink after work. She named a bar that the reporters did not frequent. But naturally, someone from my old paper was there.

"Lorraine! How have you been? What have you been doing?"

Learning how to cook. "Oh, you know my father was sick . . . his heart. He's better, and I'm just in town for a few days."

"Coming back to the paper? You know, you might get your job back. Why don't you come up and see Owen?"

"Uh, huh . . . I'm really looking elsewhere." You don't believe me, you think I had a baby, will you stop this? "Oh, there's Julie. I'm meeting her. See you."

Julie and I sat on the other side of the place. The man from my old paper was meeting a woman there, not his wife. Our encounter may have been just as embarrassing to him as it was to me. I never went back there again.

Two months or so after the Toronto fiasco, I had an interview lined up in Albany. I had run an advertisement for myself in *Editor and Publisher,* and the editor of *The Knickerbocker News* telephoned. Owen had once worked with the man and offered to put in a good word for me. Owen said he would telephone him the morning of our interview, set for noon. I did not ask specifically what Owen planned to say. And I did not want to know if the man I was going to meet knew the truth. I simply needed a job. I stopped on the road and phoned Owen, and he reported that the prospects looked good.

I was offered a job almost as soon as the interview began. The missing six months were not mentioned.

I surmised he knew the truth.

He gave me a choice of covering education or science and medicine, and I jumped at the latter because women were always being offered beats like education. My decision turned out to be better than anticipated. During the two years I was there, abortion and public assistance for health care went through the state legislature, the Dudley Observatory had some experiments on space shots, and the Albany Medical Center had a lot of fine research plus a few hospital scandals going on simultaneously. The State Health Department was ten minutes away.

Days before I began working in Albany, my father telephoned the old newspaper office and asked for me. The operator said I hadn't been there for months, she didn't know where I went. Eventually, my father was put through to Owen, who told him that I was on special assignment and was working at home. Owen telephoned me. I phoned home.

"Mom? I heard you called the paper. I've had mononucleosis, and the paper let me do some features at home. I didn't want to tell you and get you worried. I'm all right now, really everything is fine. But I've decided to move. I've taken a job in Albany."

You don't want the truth.

"No, I haven't been in trouble with a man—everything is fine, really."

She was saying that I must have been mixed up with a man. How come my telephone number was unlisted? "You're no better than a gypsy."

"I know I just moved here, but I found a better job. I know it's a smaller paper, but it is in the state capital, and I'll have a regular beat. I won't be second string on everybody's beat like I've been here."

They had discovered that something funny was going

on when a friend in Detroit telephoned them saying she had heard I was back home, taking care of my sick father.

I was only thankful that all this happened after the baby was born, after I had found another job, after Owen knew enough to cover for me.

I found an apartment in a building that resembled a motel, the kind of place you couldn't imagine anyone living in for a long time. It was partially furnished in fake colonial and had a kitchen that was no more than appliances and a sink lined up along one wall of the living room. I hated the place from the day I moved in, and nothing ever changed that. Its only attributes had been its immediate availability and proximity to work.

I threw myself into my new job. I covered science and medicine and what-have-you from 8 A.M. to late afternoon. I volunteered to write reviews. The Saratoga Performing Arts Center opened that summer, and I got assigned to cover the New York City Ballet during their month's stay there. Ballet I knew something about. I knew that I loved it.

That summer, there were lots of times when I'd work a full day, come home for an hour or so, drive up to Saratoga, get back to the office around midnight, and finish my review between one and two in the morning. And be back at work at 8 A.M. You don't have to think about much if you keep on running. Or so I thought.

Mrs. Hera had warned me that once I got settled in a new job and new place to live, and the strangeness and excitement were over, the grieving would set in all over again. I wasn't prepared for what happened.

Keith lived above me. We had moved in the same day, and so I got to know him and his girl friend right off the bat. She was a lawyer who worked in a nearby town. Keith had a year-long residency in psychiatry at the Albany Medical Center, which somehow gave me license to spill out my story to him one night over a few beers.

"Keith, I've got something really terrible to tell you about me. I . . . I . . . uh . . . I gave away a child. I had a baby a few months ago and she was adopted." I bit my lip and it began to bleed. We were sitting on the floor in Keith's place. He didn't have a couch yet. I was kneeling and rocking backward and forward on my heels. Keith put his arms around me. He said it was all right to cry. I was surprised I had told him, because I had thought I wouldn't tell anyone ever, except maybe the man I would marry, if I ever did, if it wasn't Brian. Keith prescribed amphetamines to help me get through the day. Little green and white capsules of nervous energy.

I would knock on his door and say, can we talk?

"Keith, tell me I'm not terrible, please. Tell me or I'll crack up. I never knew it would be like this. Am I crazy, or what? I feel like any minute now I can decide to step over to the other side and then you can take me to the medical center and have me committed. I can be crazy very easily. Did I tell you I had an aunt who committed suicide? It runs in the family, doesn't it?"

"Listen to me, Lorraine, you did what you had to. It's sad, but it's not such a terrible thing. You have got to convince yourself that it's not so terrible."

Oh yes it is. And did I do what I had to? Really? I don't think I can get off that easily.

He would calm me down and send me home, and I would cry myself to sleep somewhere around two or three in the morning. The next day my eyes would burn and I would drink two martinis at lunch and go back to the office and immerse myself in tracking down a story for tomorrow's paper. I ended up staying late a lot because it was easier to write when the phones stopped and most of the people were gone. Besides, what was there to do when I was through for the day?

I had to visit the company doctor. For an examination. It was a matter of policy for all new employees. He gave me an internal examination. I was rigid, nervous. He asked me to relax again and again. He asked if I had ever had a child.

"No."

At least he did not contradict me.

A few times, when I couldn't make it through the day and was desperate at noon, I would call Keith at the hospital, and we would meet on his lunch hour at the hospital's tennis courts. There was always somebody playing.

"I'm not going to have any more children. I can't. It's not fair. You keep one, you give one away."

"That's not really rational. Maybe you'll feel differently one day, but you don't have to think about it now."

"You know what someone who read my palm once said? She cupped my hand like this and looked for the children's lines—this was before I was pregnant, I think I had just met Brian but we . . . nothing was going on— and she said there was one child, but something was wrong. Like it was adopted. Do you know what I thought she meant? I thought I would adopt a child. She also said that I would make a good mother. You know what? I would have. I used to baby-sit for this little girl across the street. I used to read her stories and make up games for her, and I really liked her. I mean, I liked taking care of her too."

Consider this: I will always know what it is like to

bear a child. Nobody will ever be able to say to me, you don't know what you're talking about because *you* never had one of your own, you're a career woman. Childless and unfulfilled, you don't know what you're missing.

They are right. You don't know what you are missing until you have one. I know exactly what I am missing.

Everything changes. Everything. You become a different woman. Life looks different because now it has the feel of generations, and your own dramas become part of a larger picture, and whatever happens is always seen in perspective of how it will affect the children. There's no escaping it. Now I understand perfectly well why the world's great artists and writers are mostly men; a child can be that fulfilling. The child takes over your life, and you feel that's just how it should be. It feels right and good.

But since I don't have the child, I had better do something worth doing. Writing is not quite enough anymore. I used to rationalize that simply creating a diversion for others would be enough to make a life. That was before. My life is divided into two parts: before and After.

Keith seemed to understand, even though he was only a man. I knew I could never repay Keith for pulling me through those months, but I figured that there would be plenty of times when I would have the chance to do something for someone else.

On nights I didn't have assignments or someplace to go, the pills would wear off between eight and ten P.M., and I'd dissolve into a sobbing mass of tears and guilt and recrimination. Staring at myself in the bathroom mirror watching rivulets of mascara stream down my cheeks. Lying naked in bed, staring at my stomach, convinced that it was moving, breathing, heart beating. I felt like I was on one of those carnival rides with two giant arms that swoop around: up all day, then a gut-shaking fall where all sense of equilibrium was gone. I stopped taking the pills.

A scaly patch of dry skin, red and itchy, appeared on my leg. It covered the back of my knee and half the front. It spread to my right hand. Keith said the eruption was undoubtedly caused by an emotional reaction. He prescribed cortisone cream, and I wore a white gauze bandage around my leg and on my hand for months. The sore wouldn't go away and somehow I felt it was fitting, that the world could see the degradation.

Now Keith prescribed tranquilizers. I didn't like to take them. I hated the drugged stupor. Being alive means feeling.

A month, then two, went by.

Brian would call now and then and mostly on Friday afternoons. He continued to say "I'll come for you," but he did not say when. I did not ask. I began telling myself at odd moments of the night and day that I had to start living as if Brian would never come for me. I would imagine myself, years later, wizened and dry, still waiting. I tried not to think of the fact that if we did end up together, it would somehow be unfair to the child, the one who got away.

I started seeing other men. Albany had its fair share of eligible men, not only reporters from the local papers, but also the press corps from all over the state, and various aides and what-have-you that are all part of the legislative process, mostly male.

I was a scared rabbit. I had the best intentions: I didn't want to hurt anyone. I didn't want to say no when logic told me I should say yes, yet I found myself getting jumpy and persnickety and walking away and my companion wondering what had happened to upset me when there wasn't the slightest indication that anything was wrong. I was afraid of being alone and I was afraid of getting involved. I was afraid of change, I was afraid of things staying the same. I'm not too pleased with the way I was then. I wasn't honest. I'd say one thing and not quite mean it. The most important thing was to keep running, to not look back.

To add to the confusion, I wore Brian's gold· band on my wedding finger. I hadn't taken it off. If asked about it, I offered no explanation. "No," I would say, "no, I am not married." There was nothing to add.

The child was everywhere. True, I stopped thinking about her every hour, and maybe sometimes several days would manage to slip by when she didn't come floating into my mind. But then something: forsythia painted on a greeting card, baby clothes in a store window, commercials for gentle Ivory Snow, safe for baby; my mother writing to ask what I wanted her to do with a dress she'd made for me when I was six or seven, a sheer pale blue with lace and ruffles; the gold pin my father gave me that once belonged to his mother; people coming out of church after a wedding, and I'd just happened to be driving by and catch the look on the bride's face; an announcement from a cousin of her new baby's christening. All of these things would fill the secret pockets of my heart and head and say: fallen woman who gave her child away. I began to understand fully what it means to live with one of those things that time would never heal.

I would always be a woman who gave away a child.

My parents came to visit in the summer. I had the bandage on my leg and I had gained twenty pounds. I had been eating like a mad woman. They said, what's wrong, are you all right, you look funny? My mother said she did not believe I had mono. Over and over again. Whenever we were alone. I told her she had to believe me; I said it straight out and harsh, there was no other way. If she didn't believe me, it was her problem. They washed my venetian blinds and put up my drapes and said so that's how it is, everything besides your work comes second, do all your friends work as hard as you?

Another month and more went by.

Brian got there in September. On Thursday afternoon as I was clearing up my desk, he called from the highway and said he would be at my place in little more than an hour. He said he had taken the day off from work, but Kathleen didn't know that. "I'm coming to you." I ran home and showered and stuffed nylons in drawers and smoothed out the couch.

I watched from a window as he got out of his car and walked to the door. He was wearing a crisp blue-and-white seersucker suit; he was not smiling. I could feel my heart on overload. I knew what he had said and now here he was at my doorstep, but I couldn't believe this was actually happening. A flash flood of sweat engulfed me; I was clammy everywhere.

Instead of being happy, we both were strange. He was there, all right. But now what? I would beg. If he had come this far, I would pull out all the stops to make him stay. He arrived before sunset, and we talked until nearly dawn. We ate an omelet in a diner and drove back to the place where it all began.

We checked into a motel, the kind with orange leatherette sofas and cigarette burns in the Formica table-tops. He went to the office after a few hours' sleep. I went for a walk. He said he would call his wife and see her after work. He would tell her. Was this actually happening? Would I be Brian's lady officially? Would we be man and wife? I put my belief on hold. I would believe it when it happened.

He said that Kathleen cried and professed to know nothing of the affair. She begged him not to leave. What about the children? It was as much her fault as his and couldn't they try again?

He did not tell her about our child.

Why?

That night, Brian had bad dreams and kept waking up in his sleep, covered with sweat and making sounds that reminded me of the voices in my dream. I had to turn on the light a few times so that he would calm down.

The next night we had dinner in a restaurant with his brother, who, up until this time, knew nothing of me. He was as polite as possible, considering that he told Brian that he was making a big mistake.

"This will kill Mother." She was as Irish and as Catholic as they make them.

"Kathleen doesn't deserve this." Tell him about our baby, because he's going to bring the children up next.

"And of course I won't point out that you've got three young kids." *Four.*

Looking back on it now, I don't see how I sat through the meal, but we were civil to one another and somehow I walked away feeling that his brother wasn't such a bad guy. He was only doing what he thought best. Brian said that his mother would take it hard, but she would be all right once the storm passed, and someday when I got to know her, everything would be fine. "She's quite a woman," he said. "Like you."

On Sunday, I took a bus back to Albany. On Monday, Brian went out of town to cover a Democratic state convention, which meant a week of little sleep, lots of booze, and writing for deadlines after the politicians had finally turned out the lights. Brian called at least once a day.

On Saturday afternoon, I was home waiting for his call. He was back at the office writing his column. His kids were calling him on the telephone. *Daddy, when are you coming home?* He was exhausted and he had a suitcase full of dirty shirts. He had no place to go.

He called me and said he couldn't do it.

I did not remind him that we were rare. That would not be enough. I did not try to change his mind. I had lost Brian to the way things were, and I knew by the defeat in his voice that there was nothing to do but retreat and hang up. We might always be rare, but we would never be together.

I started to black out, but put my head down between my legs in time to stop the starry images floating in. I called a girl friend from the paper, who knew nothing of the affair or the child, and said I had to come over right away.

I got into my car and drove straight through a stop sign at the corner. Another car barely missed hitting me sideways. The driver got out of his car and swore at me. I said I was sorry, there had just been a death in the family. If he had hit me, I might have died.

It did not seem like such a bad idea.

9

Work, Love, and She Turns One

The job in Albany turned out to be the kind I'd dreamed about since I first wanted to be a newspaper reporter, when I was twelve or thirteen. Maybe I had decided to become a reporter because I wasn't pretty, and I figured that I'd always have to take care of myself; maybe because I liked running around talking to people I wouldn't get a chance to meet otherwise; maybe because I liked the idea of what a reporter is; maybe because *The Free Press* carried Brenda Starr; maybe because my father read three newspapers a day; and probably for all of these reasons together. And now, the right job had dropped into my lap. I would learn how to do it right in Albany, and then I would move on to a bigger city, a more prestigious newspaper. Like *The New York Times.*

There were other women on the city staff when I got there, and others followed soon enough, covering the courts and politics and education. "Dusky, get up here," is the way Pete on the city desk would get my attention. I loved it. We all did.

It hadn't fazed me when I started covering science and medicine that the only D I'd ever got in college was in physics, and the only biology I had ever had was in high school, and I hadn't exactly been a star pupil. I wasn't going to do the research. After all, my job was to understand what was going on and then translate that to the readers. I would ask enough questions until I was sure I had it right, and then I would phone up the doctors and read them their quotes. This wasn't obstructing the truth, it was only helping me to get the story straight.

The public relations officer of the Albany Medical Center was quite specific about his reaction to me: "You're the new medical writer? This is who the *Knick* sends me? What are you? Twenty? Where did you go to school?"

"St. Alphonsus Elementary. The nuns told me I should be a writer. And I'm really a very old fifteen."

"I ask for a reporter and I get Little Red Riding Hood."

"Well, we don't have to wonder who the wolf is."

By the end of the summer, we were friends, or at least, sparring partners: "Listen, Jack the Ripper, I heard that there's a revolt brewing on the board of trustees to get rid of the director. Anything you want to say about that? Officially or on the QT? But I suppose in that ivory tower guarded by an assistant and a secretary, you haven't heard anything. No, I won't tell you where I heard it. I keep my secrets."

"Listen, Polack, could I interest you in a story about our new heart monitoring equipment?"

"Next week, maybe. I'm serious about this. You've got an hour to call me back. Or read about it in the morning. 'A spokesman for the hospital declined to comment. . . .'"

There were lots of good stories to cover in Albany. Public assistance for the medical bills of the needy was being debated in the legislature—and by the state chapter of the American Medical Association, who railed against such wholesale medicine. Or was it their incomes they were talking about? Doctors normally love coverage, but they threw me out of a meeting on the issue. I went into the banquet room next to theirs, found a closet between the two rooms, and shut the door behind me. There was a heater of some sort in the closet, along with mops and pails, and it got awfully hot. I took off my shoes and stripped to my slip.

I knew enough big guns in the organization to recognize their voices as they spoke, and I took careful notes. No calling to check quotes today. And if I was going to name names, I had better be right than sued. I phoned the city desk at noon, stayed in the ladies' room during the lunch recess (I was afraid if they saw me they would get wind of what I was doing), and snuck back to my closet as soon as they were in session again. The story, with pictures from our files, was splashed across the second front the next morning. No one contradicted my quotes, but everyone asked how I got them. Of course I didn't tell because I might need the little room again.

Abortion was going through the state legislature, and I was sent to the capitol to cover a public hearing. Anyone could have made good copy out of the impassioned pleas, the photographs of fetuses, and the wire coat hangers brandished about that day. A few weeks later, I holed up in the library, interviewed thirty or fifty people, and wrote a four-part series that ran on the front page. I noted that the Catholic Church had been ambivalent about its position in the early days. Even St. Thomas Aquinas said only that abortion was a sin after "the quickening," whenever that was. The Church's lobbyist called me to complain and wanted to know why I was taking on Catholicism. I know all about the Catholic Church, I said. It's a lot easier to criticize something if you are an insider.

I sent copies of the series to *Cosmopolitan* and asked if they would like a story. I got a postcard saying no.

Dudley Observatory had an experiment set for a Gemini space shot, and over the discouragement and disbelief of everyone except the editor-in-chief and the city editor, I wrote a memo to the publisher explaining why he should spend close to a thousand dollars to send me to Houston. Dudley's part consisted of small boxes collecting impressions of space dust as the module whizzed along.

I went to the NASA space center, and afterward I went to the White Sands missile base in New Mexico where Dudley was firing some rockets. Then it was back to Texas, this time to a small town called Palestine, where Dudley and the weather bureau launched a balloon. One of the researchers from Dudley and I tracked it all night in a single-engine airplane, setting down in Birmingham, Alabama, where we ran out of gas. It was four A.M. I tried to sleep on the ladies' room floor. The first plane to Atlanta, my connection back to Albany, left at seven. I had filed my stories by telephone at odd hours of the night throughout the week. When I got back, the Hearst Corporation honored me for the best spot news coverage of the month. And later, my stories won the annual award for same.

Another time, Bobby Kennedy and a retinue of at least twenty people—wife, sisters, in-laws, kids, friends, etcetera—were going white water canoeing on a stretch of the Hudson River a few hours' north of Albany. Associated Press sent a Pulitzer Prize winning photographer just back from Vietnam, the reporter would come from Albany, and it was me. I think I got the assignment simply because I was still in the office late Friday afternoon. I had at least fifteen minutes to pack my long underwear before the photographer picked me up at home. To get part of the story, we cajoled a hunting guide to take us alongside the river where the group would be coming by. The hunter didn't want to take me. "Do you know what it's like out there? I mean, it's no *damn* tea party. It's rough country. She won't be able to keep up." I was standing right there. I told him I exercised at home.

I don't remember what convinced him to let me come along, except that I kept saying that I was strong enough. It turned out that the photographer was the one who couldn't keep up.

He insisted the terrain—we were walking on a fairly steep incline, with plenty of growth and no trails—was more difficult than Vietnam. He asked me to carry two of his five or six cameras. His pictures and my story ran on the AP wire. Given the chance, it was quite easy to be taken seriously as a reporter, regardless of the fact that I usually wore a skirt. Perhaps the best compliment of all came when the AP staffer would stop by my desk in the morning after he went through the carbons of the stories that would be running next edition. He was just making sure I didn't have a hot story working that he didn't know about. A note from another reporter found on your typewriter in the morning saying, What a good job yesterday, makes the late nights, the missed dinners, the deadline tension all worthwhile. The respect of your peers is one of the things that counts the most in this business.

But as I got better at my job and had more than a passing share of good assignments, some of my friends— well, one woman in particular—put distance between us, saying unfriendly things. I don't think it had anything to do with the child; she had been sympathetic when I told her. I chalked her new coolness up to my raging ambition, but such rejections always hurt and make you question what's wrong with yourself. Was I overly aggressive? Had I stolen a story from anyone? I didn't think so. Had I hurt anyone, left bodies in my wake? No. Would it have been different if I were a man?

The hospital knew I was the right woman to send the bills to. I would have a day of relative calm, and when I got home from work, a bill for the extra charges for the incubator would be lying in wait in the mailbox, ready to pounce.

There were still a few hundred dollars due. Brian had paid most of the hospital charges, borrowing money so Kathleen wouldn't know, but the additional cost for the incubator was more than we could handle at the time. We paid half; we would take care of the rest later. And so the bills followed me from one town to the next. If only they had contained some news of her, how welcome they would have been.

I would rip one open and stare at the letters and numbers as if they were written in code, hiding information on her whereabouts and well-being.

Was she sickly? Was she strong? Was she crawling yet? Did they hold her and say big words for her to imitate, the way my daddy did for me? Was she still alive? Or had she died, a victim of crib death? Just last week I read a story about a little girl who had mysteriously died in her crib, no one knew why.

I poured myself a glass of wine.

This wasn't what I'd planned on at all: reading stories about crib death and wondering about my little girl.

I can pinch myself, I know I am alive.

I went to the telephone and called Keith, or anyone. I wanted to laugh, to drink a glass or three of wine, to talk about anything and try to forget, at least for the night.

"Lorraine, why won't you go to bed with me? What's wrong? Everything is fine, and then you pull back. Are you afraid? Of what?" Another reporter is speaking. We had been dating a few months. He is not married. Not having to sneak around was quite nice. Also, being able to see him on Saturday night.

"I guess I am afraid. I don't know why . . . it's not you. It's me." I can't, I can't, I can't. If I do, I am no better than a slut. Maybe that's already true and what difference does it make anyhow? I am dirt.

"I'm sorry, really I am. I'd better go now. You don't have to see me out."

I was having a hard time. If you weren't sexually liberated in those years, you were uptight and out-of-touch, an old maid no matter how short you wore your skirts. With the possibility of pregnancy no longer a good excuse for saying no to almost every sexual advance that happened along, a lot of women said *yes,* as if the question were no more important than how you wanted your eggs. There was also the matter of the double standard: To deal it a death blow, it was necessary to join in the revolution, without questioning feelings too harshly every step of the way. Romance was not supposed to be necessary to enjoy a good, clean, athletic tussle in the sheets; healthy one-night stands were celebrated. But it wasn't quite that simple, for women are always looking for romance with sex, and if the romance isn't there, they make it up, eight times out of ten. The programming is in the genes and isn't likely to change overnight, or in a few decades. Women have the babies. We know we need partners and babies need fathers.

One weekend at the end of winter, when the snow was melting and the crocuses pushing through, this reporter and I flew to Washington to visit friends of his from South Dakota. They worked for Senator George McGovern. The three of them spent the weekend talking about people I would never know and politics I didn't care about. I spent the weekend playing with their seven-year-old daughter. She was blonde. They remarked on how well we got along.

That was the last weekend I went anywhere with him. I later heard that he said I was too distant, that you couldn't get to know me, that I kept changing my mind. He said I was . . . ah, messed up. I had told him about the child.

Brian wrote and said he missed me, told me I was knocking 'em dead with my stories. He would sign off "I love you," and he would enclose twenty dollars for the hospital bills. He telephoned now and then, but not frequently. We made no mention of what would not be. No future in that. I asked him how things were going, and he said that he was teaching Kathleen to play chess.

When the forsythia came again, my daughter turned one. I do not specifically remember the day. I had begun to put her away in corners of my mind where I did not ruminate daily or dally long, where the dust began to gather on the pain. Weeks and days beforehand, I remember thinking, soon it will be her birthday, how am I going to live through the day? On the actual date, it never crossed my mind. Weeks later when I remembered, I was taken aback because I had so coolly missed it, and felt guilty that I had not spent the day in mourning.

But I think that forgetting was kind of sweet salvation. It had become necessary to dull the cutting edge of memory if I was ever going to be able to pick up the pieces of a life gone haywire. I wanted to survive, and I realized that I could still be screaming in a hospital somewhere. When I began to recognize how truly sick I had been that first year, I knew that I was getting well.

That spring, the New York chapter of the American Medical Association and the New York State Health Department gave me three hundred dollars and a plaque for my wall attesting to the fact that I had achieved a certain excellence in medical reporting. I went to New York City to accept the award, and my picture was taken with some of the doctors I'd covered that day from the closet.

Who's Who of American Women sent me a form to fill out. It occurred to me that if my daughter ever found out my name, she could trace me through it. But I would not let it show that there had been a six-month lapse in my life. I couldn't admit that to the world, as if anyone would have noticed. Or cared. Now my concern seems absurd. But when the edition appeared, all the time was accounted for.

My mother told me that Harry was proud of me, showed my stories to the neighbors. Took them with him when he visited his brothers. Talked about me with pride and some amazement. That daughter of his had done all right for herself.

I decided it was time to get my nose fixed. With the money from the award (the hospital bill was now completely paid) and an insurance policy, I had the extra thousand I needed for the operation. I had wanted to have the bump removed and the length shortened ever since it cropped out in adolescence. I'd even ferreted away the name of the plastic surgeon our family doctor recommended when I was fifteen.

For years I had convinced myself that the deformity —and it was that—was good for me. People used to stare at me, I could feel their eyes drifting down from mine when we first met. It would make me strong, make me sensitive, make me a better person, a better writer. When I saw *Fahrenheit 451* and watched the happy people having their bandages removed on the wall screen—now they looked just like everybody else—I vowed never to tamper with my exterior. But suddenly, all of the rationalizations were found to be simply that. I was tired of being called "nosy." I was tired of having a face with which the rest of me didn't feel synchronized. I was tired of men saying, after they got to know me: "I never knew you were so charming." I have smiled at that remark more than I am pleased to admit. And that Christmas, a little girl without a mean bone in her body stared at me and said in the softest possible voice, "You have a big nose." I know, I said.

I got it fixed a few months later.

I have never had a sorry day. I didn't even get the customary black-and-blue marks; and afterward, my mother remarked that now I looked like a cousin. She'd never seen the resemblance before.

Did life get easier with the new nose?

Do you have to ask?

In Albany, I began reading *The New York Times* as if it were a journalism primer. It was the best, wasn't it? The *Times* became the standard against which I judged my stories. I knew I wanted to work for it. Succeed in New York, and you don't ever have to prove yourself again.

The first time I'd gone to New York I had been a senior in college. That year I had a scholarship, and so I had a few dollars to splurge. A girl friend and I took an all-night express bus from Detroit, stayed at a hotel in Brooklyn, and got discount tickets to as many shows as we could cram into a week. We changed our shoes and freshened up for the night in the ladies' room of the main branch of the public library on Fifth Avenue. I fell unabashedly in love with New York City.

This was Big Town, where I wanted to make it, but I was afraid of saying that outright: What if I wasn't good enough? What if father was right? It was hard to get a reporter's job. What if I failed? Somehow, Chicago or Boston or Philadelphia seemed easier worlds to conquer. But Albany made me think I could come to New York.

I began besieging the *Times* city editor with letters and clips, and he kept writing back that there are no openings, The *World Journal Tribune* has just folded, and we are swamped with applicants. Please write again at some unspecified date. Try as I might, I could not get an interview. I did not try the women's editor—until a *Times* reporter I met in Albany pleaded my case with her. I wrote, and she agreed to see me.

At the *Times,* I was paraded around to seven or eight assorted editors. I met the publisher, and I met the city editor, the one who had turned me down. He looked at me and said, "Oh, it's you. Maybe you could work down here . . . but I guess if you're here for Charlotte it's really too late for that." I didn't even flinch. I had been convincing myself and the women's editor that the features in her department were exactly the kind I was dying to write, and I had stopped questioning that. It was *The New York Times,* wasn't it?

After two days of interviews, and a night on her couch, I was told to go back to Albany and keep up the good work, keep sending her clips. Maybe someday, not soon, there would be a place for me.

I made one other foray into New York journalism, this one to NBC local news. The lone woman was being promoted to national news; local would be replacing *her*. The NBC crew in Albany put the bug in my ear and arranged for an interview in New York. I bought a tape recorder and worked on modulating my voice and cleaning up the excess "uhhs." The interview seemed to go fine, but I wasn't offered an on-camera audition, and word came from my friends that the woman hired would be from a minority group. Other than female, that is. I was too blonde and too all-American.

The men had their tight little club and let women in sparingly, if at all. And then, you had better be damn good; in fact you had to be better than most of the men if you didn't want them saying, Not bad for a woman. I never wanted to hear that; I vowed I would work hard enough and be good enough so that I never would. It sounds as if I am talking about another century, but it was little more than a decade ago.

I took it all in stride. I insisted on playing the game, and these were the rules. I would make it in spite of them.

What else had I fought for?

10

A Different Drummer

At the end of the second summer in Albany, I took a week's vacation on Nantucket. There is something about an island that rejuvenates me as much as if I were on a retreat. Almost without noticing it, I begin a general housecleaning, sopping up the detritus of a life cluttered with detail. I prefer to come and go by boat; that way, there can be no doubt that this place is not the same as the place from which I came. Anyway, on this trip, I intended to write bleak poetry. That I did.

I do not think that I wanted to meet someone, but I did, and so I must have been ready. I have to admit that when I'm not looking forward to being with someone, I am not looking forward to much. I used to try and convince myself that this wasn't the case, but I have given up in the face of cold fact. It is the way I thrive, and that's all there is to it.

Ben was five years younger than I; he was entering his

junior year in college, which made him nineteen the year we met. He picked me up in town my first evening there by coming right up to me and asking if I believed in vibrations. He said he had been waiting to see if I would walk by three times; and if I did, he said, then he'd just walk up and find something to say.

He was innocent and sweet and endearingly naïve, the antithesis of everything I felt about myself. He added a year to his age and bought me a cup of coffee, and I was hooked right from the beginning. He had been on Nantucket all summer, working at a huge old place called the Sea Cliff Inn. It's been torn down since.

He invited me down to his homecoming weekend in the fall. I went on a quick-weight-loss-diet and shed twelve pounds. I bought a navy-blue pleated skirt, knee socks, and loafers and arrived on campus in my yellow convertible Karmann Ghia. It was the perfect weekend. I worked on his fraternity's float, we went to a lot of parties, and our team won the game. I hadn't done these things in college myself, and now I was being given the chance.

Two weeks later, Ben came to Albany, and although I know this doesn't sound logical, he fit right into my life: friends, job, apartment, everything. On the last day, we were driving to a restaurant on the top of a mountain. It was a Sunday in November, clear and crisp.

"We might as well get married" was how he put it.

I looked out the window. Vivid patches of color whizzed by. I must tell him. Now.

"I had a child. I mean, an illegitimate child. The father was married, and I gave her up for adoption."

"So? That doesn't change anything. I said, do you want to get married?"

"Of course." He will never desert me, I know it.

"I think we should talk about kids," he continued. "I don't want any. Not ever."

"That's fine with me. I don't see how I can work, really, and take care of kids. When I was young, I never thought I would have children." But I did, and that changes everything. I can't keep one and give one away. It's not fair.

"I am positive I don't want children," he repeated. "The first time I ever thought about it I was in the drugstore with my father, and he said something about 'when you have your own son.' I said right then, 'I'm not going to have kids.' He said, 'Aw, you'll change your mind one day.' and I said I wouldn't. We dropped the matter. But I never changed my mind. I don't want to be a professional baseball player, and I don't have to try it first to know it's not for me. I feel the same way about children. I don't need to have any to know I don't want them."

His parents were less than thrilled about the marriage. They offered him a camping trip across the country, and then a car, and then a grand tour of Europe with his best friend, *and* a car. Some of my friends questioned what I was doing. I was too sophisticated. He was too young. I announced the news to my parents at Christmas. They were relieved. My father was a bit cautious about the age difference, but I think he had given up opposing me, since it had never seemed to do much good anyway.

I know now how desperately I needed that marriage. It would validate me as a legitimate person, worthy to have in your home, a normal, healthy, functioning member of society, not the imposter I felt like underneath.

See, I can be just like everybody else. Marriage would somehow launder away the stain of what I had done. It would give me society's stamp of approval. Also my mother's. It was turning out that her endorsement was

more important than I had expected. I wanted her for-
giveness for a sin she didn't know I had committed. Some
of these thoughts may have been whispering around my
brain, but I didn't let them get far, and I concentrated on
the love I felt between Ben and me.

We made plans to get married during his spring vacation. We would have waited longer, but his parents' re-
lentless opposition prevented that.

And then my father died. He had a heart attack, and
he died before he got to the hospital. I was dressed and
ready to leave for work when the call came. As soon as
I heard my mother's sobbing voice, I knew.

I wanted to get married more than ever. You could
say I was getting married on the rebound, but I am not
sure from what. Everything was slipping through my
fingers.

Daddy, I had a little girl. There's a whole new generation in our family now, and you don't even know it. It's
best this way. You would have been sad for me if you
knew. You would have been disappointed too. Daddy, I
just couldn't admit to what a botch I've made of things.
Daddy, I won't let you down. I swear I'll make you proud.

We went ahead with the wedding plans.

I called Brian from Albany just before I flew home
to Dearborn. He was no longer at the newspaper; he had
taken a higher paying job with the city as part of the fix-up-
his-marriage plan. A secretary answered his phone. "Miss
Who? Does he know what this is in reference to?"

We chatted, we were polite. He told me he was happy
for me, that things seemed to be working out. I did not
want him to say anything about us, on the one hand, and on
the other hand, I did. I had no idea what I would do if he

said anything other than Congratulations. He didn't, and I contentedly went home and got married, with champagne and a homemade wedding cake. I suppose I could have worn white, but I chose not to, for it seemed as if I had already been someone's bride. Wasn't I already someone's mother?

I picked a dress off the rack at Macy's—a pink crepe reminiscent of the thirties—and wore a gardenia in my hair. Gardenias are so terrifically potent, and then they're gone. They are my mother's favorite flower.

The only trouble was the dreams: my father, shadowy, with feet that melded into the ground, standing next to a tree. He was part of the tree at the roots and he was asking me to come join him. To kill myself to be with him.

I kept up my correspondence with *The New York Times,* and I also applied for a job on the small daily in the town where Ben's school was. After all, he still had a year of school left. The publisher was incredulous when I told him that I was also applying for a job on the *Times* and would come to work for him if I didn't get it. Ben and I found an apartment that would be available in the fall.

I quit the *Knick* in May, and Ben and I went to Nantucket for the summer. Ben got his old job as general all-around-everything at the Sea Cliff Inn, and I was taken on as the hostess in the dining room. The Sea Cliff Inn was a romantic, crumbling gray castle of a place, the kind where Hitchcock might show up any moment.

And in the middle of that magical summer of swimming and sunning and working seven days a week, I got a letter from the *Times* women's editor saying that maybe I wasn't ready yet. I wrote back and suggested two story ideas I could research while I was there. She waited a few weeks before writing back to tell me I had the job. And so when September came, Ben went to school, and I went to *The New York Times*. Everything was turning out all right, wasn't it? But that first year wasn't any fun at all; I missed Ben, there wasn't enough money, and the job turned out to be hell.

I was assigned to cover a story on how wild panty hose would be for the spring. I was assigned to make a story out of the rising cost and everlasting durability of elephant leather as sold through a pricy boutique for white hunters and their women. I was sent to interview a couple who were fringe royalty of some sort, to determine if they had a story worth telling; not exactly to write a story, but to check the lay of the land, the juiciness of the quotes; I shouldn't be disappointed if nothing came of it. I was told to call a high priestess of fashion and society and find out if she and her friends were seriously thinking of opening a boutique. The women's editor, of course, would be writing the story, or at least making it a line in the one she was working on. She needed the dope before I went home. I had no idea how to get that unlisted number, but a woman who sat near me—and knew the person I was trying to reach—opened her phone book and read it to me. What amazed me is that when I tracked down this estimable personage, she turned out to be en route from New York to Washington, D.C., and she actually telephoned me from National Airport to quash the rumor. Such is the power of *The New York Times*. I was quickly made aware how the magic phrase "I'm from the *Times*" opens doors and commands disproportionate respect. People smile and invite you in for a drink. The job turned out to be not my best event.

I interviewed the wife of a conservative candidate for the Senate. The couple had several children, but they hadn't had any for the last few years. They were Catholic. When I turned in my story, I was soundly dressed down by a particularly rabid liberal on the copy desk for not finding out if the couple practiced birth control—naturally, against the tenets of their religion. "I'm going to get him," he said.

While I was on the paper, I had a rare assignment or two that I thoroughly enjoyed. One was a story on the house that Charlie Brown built, a Murray Hill residence that was being lovingly restored by the young producer of the the off-Broadway play based on the characters from the comic strip. The other was a story on the welfare department's homemakers, women who came into your house and took care of the children while the family was going through some kind of trouble. I wrote about a family in the Bronx; the mother had been badly burned in a grease fire while cooking.

Those stories notwithstanding, it is an understatement to say that the job was not turning out well. Hired as one of the youngest full-fledged reporters and given a starting salary commensurate with five years' experience when I was only four years out of college, I was under tremendous pressure to prove I had the goods. I was under the gun and unable to relax, because with the kind of stories I was assigned, I couldn't prove anything.

There was also the atmosphere of the place; it wasn't like any other newspaper I'd ever been on. People were tense, nervous, worried; if you got into the dog house because you blew an assignment, it was awfully hard to get out because good assignments weren't coming your way anymore. Or at least for a while. The women's page was grossly overstaffed. I believe I counted nineteen reporters all vying for space on the page. It was supposed to make for "creative tension." If your story was bumped for someone else's, feelings of brotherly love came hard. And remember, these are not people who take themselves or their jobs casually; these are "the best," the most aggressive, the most ambitious. I never heard it then, but I understand now why some of the old timers call it the Velvet Coffin. Was this what I had been training for most of my life?

Because of all the tension, half of the reporters seemed worried about the other half doing them in. There were cliques within cliques; the place was electric with jealousy. However, it wasn't unrelieved horror, for the women I sat near and one or two others were friendly and helpful and did what they could to get me going in the right direction.

Simple friendship wasn't enough.

I lasted four months, the length of my trial period. Being told that "things weren't working out" has turned out to be a blessing, but only in retrospect. At the time, it absolutely flattened me, just as a steam roller would have. This job was supposed to be the capstone of my career, the place I'd work forever. It was what I had been gearing up for since at least the ninth grade when I got on the staff of the *Excalibur* at Sacred Heart High and decided I liked the newspaper business just fine. And now the dream was over. Kaput. Everything had turned to ashes. I didn't have my baby, and I didn't have the job. For years, I couldn't admit—even to close friends—precisely what had happened. I was vague about my *New York Times* experience. Very vague. One friend found out the truth when she brought up my name at a dinner party. A reporter from the women's department who was also there was only too happy to set everyone straight.

I didn't have time to sit around and lick my wounds, however. I had a husband to support. I couldn't pull up stakes and leave town this time, what with tuition and room and board to pay. Ben and I didn't consider my moving to his town and seeing if that job was still there; half of the year was already gone. I didn't apply at any of the other New York City newspapers because somehow it didn't make any sense to go from what I thought was the ultimate to second best. I ended up in the public relations department of Clairol. I was blonde and all-American enough to sell hair coloring.

I lasted little over a year; I quit when I was offered a job on a new daily that was being put together in the city. We put out a dummy issue to attract advertisers, but the last big piece of financing that would have made the operation viable didn't come through. Ben was out of school now, and so I didn't have to rush out and find another job.

I decided to try free-lancing. More specifically, I would write an article about a woman who gave away a child. I was sure that I would be able to publish the piece, since I had never seen anything on the topic before. Edith Wharton's *The Old Maid* certainly couldn't count as competition. I would write the piece anonymously. I was adamant about keeping my secret, and whenever I told someone with whom I had become intimate, my heart would beat rapidly. It was terrible, wasn't it? And my family must not ever know. I got away with it once, and I would keep it that way. My mother doesn't even have to be burdened with this hurt, I reasoned. My mother never has to know.

"Lorraine, that Kraus boy down the street, the one who goes to the University of Michigan—he's got mono," my mother said.

I was home at Christmas, as usual. "Oh, yeah?" I was reading the newspaper and not paying much attention.

"Well, he had it and was walking around and didn't know what was wrong for weeks, why he felt so tired all the time. He finally went to the doctor, and they put him in the hospital."

"Hmmm . . ."

"Was it like that when you had it? Did you get real sick? Did you know you had it?"

"Oh? Yeah. *What?*"

But if I kept the secret from my mother, I couldn't keep my daughter out of my head. How is she? Where is she? What does she look like? What does she like to do? What are her favorite foods? Does she have many friends? Can she read? Does she have brothers and sisters? See that little girl, isn't she about as old as my daughter would be?

Why do they tell me that I can never know? Why do they think it's best this way? For whom? I can't believe it would be such a crime if we met. I would never do anything to hurt her.

This endless silence is the worst of all.

Never knowing is the hardest part.

You don't forget, you just stop crying every day.

All those highfalutin experts with their hot air opinions. They don't know what they are talking about. Who among them has given away a child?

They'd change their tune. They'd change The Law.

I was positive the story would find a home; I only had to tell it. And I wasn't alone: What had happened to me had happened to millions of other women. So I was stunned when it was turned down by a woman's magazine I considered abreast of the times. After all, if lovemaking without marriage was a permissible topic, certainly the consequences would be too. The rejection letter explained nothing.

My husband was there when it came. I was also

stunned by his reaction: "You might as well face it, you're not going to make it." I am sure he was only saying that so I wouldn't get hurt again, wouldn't have to endure the frustration of further rejection, but it sounded like my father telling me I couldn't go to college. Maybe, like my father, he thought I was only setting myself up for a fall. Maybe he was bothered because I must have seemed obsessed with writing about a child from another union, a part of my life with which he had nothing to do. And maybe he was afraid of my succeeding. What would he do with me then?

I am going to have to leave you one day. You are always saying. "When you leave me," and I have always hated that. Remember how I told you never to say it again? But now I know I will leave. Not today. Sometime later. But the most important thing is, I must get the word out. Don't you see, one day maybe she'll read it, and maybe she'll call.

Make a new life? Make another joke. The new life reverberates with her. It would have been easier to lose a leg.

Ben and I were divorced a few years later. He lives in a cabin in the woods. We send each other friendly letters at Christmas. I have no way of knowing how much the child affected us; all that seemed apparent to me is that we grew apart rather than together.

Other relationships have come undone over the same issue. Of course, nothing is ever that clear-cut or simple; there are always a lot of reasons why someone who is fine one season doesn't fit in the next. But I've heard it again and again: Give up the writing. Give up the mania about your child. Put it away, you're only hurting yourself.

Once I heard it just as another someone and I had finished the dishes after dinner at his place.

"I don't think you can do it" is what this one said.

I put on my bracelet and wristwatch and walked out the door.

No one can hurt me more than I have already hurt myself.

I may look normal, but there's something a bit off. I cry much too easily, for starters.

I am a mother without a child.

11

A Roomful of Crazy People

One day I came upon a story in *The New York Times* about a group of adoptees who were trying to change the laws so that they could locate their natural parents. In virtually every state, the records were sealed by law. The group had been founded by a woman named Florence Fisher. In the story (which incidentally ran on the woman's page) Florence spoke about how she felt when she was in an accident and the doctor in the emergency room tried to get a medical history from her. What information could she give about her parents?

There was an address in the paper. I wrote and said I was doing a story on adoption and could we arrange an interview? When I got there, I told Florence that my interest in the subject was personal, and she said she had suspected; there was something about my questions, the tone of my voice.

I became a member of the Adoptees Liberty Move-

ment Association, more commonly known as ALMA—
which, Florence likes to remind everyone, is Spanish for
soul. I went to a monthly meeting. It was quite a day.
Here is what I heard:

"You can't find your daughter now, she is too young.
What is she? Five? You have to leave her alone, you have
to believe that she is all right with her parents. You have
to let her grow up and you will have to wait."

I met a few people who didn't believe I should wait.
"I wanted to meet my mother ever since I knew I was
adopted, when I was a little girl. A man came to the
house once, and I think he was my real uncle, and then
he went away, and I never saw him again. I wanted to run
away and find him because he would know where my
mother was."

"My parents don't know I'm here today. They would
die. I told them I was going shopping in the city today.
They don't understand. I never felt close to them. I'm
just not like them at all."

"I almost died when I had an operation. They couldn't
wake me up after the anesthesia, even though it was the
usual dose. It might have been different if I had known
that I had to be careful about that sort of thing."

"When my baby was born, do you know what it was
like to see for the first time a face that looked like mine?
To actually know a person I was related to?"

"When I went to the agency and told them what I
wanted they acted as if I were disturbed. The woman
went to get my file and had it open right in front of me.

No, she couldn't tell me anything. She had everything *right in front of her,* and she told me I should seek psychiatric help. I was so angry I wanted to punch her!"

"I've heard that too. 'This is not the problem, there is something else wrong, and you are using this to hide from yourself. . . .' I get so mad, I could scream. My parents were paying for therapy for three years before I simply refused to go anymore. He had me feeling that I was crazy, that wanting to know was ungrateful—here they were, paying for therapy, after all. My mother and I still can't talk about the fact that I was adopted. No, I didn't have any brothers or sisters."

"You know what I heard? If you are searching for your other parents, you must be unhappy with your adoptive parents, and you won't admit that to yourself. He said I wouldn't find an identity just because I met this woman. I'm not looking for an identity. There is just something missing the way it is now. I simply would like to know my story, what happened, how come I was adopted."

"Of course I don't want to find my mother in terrible circumstances. That's what everybody always says—maybe it is better to not know, what if you find her a prostitute? What if I do? That's not a nice story, but at least it's mine. Maybe I could help her."

"I just want to find out who I am. If she doesn't want me to bother her after that, I won't. I don't want to hurt her."

"I think I know who my daughter is. I wrote her a letter, but she didn't answer it. I have waited in front of her apartment building a few times, and once I saw her come out with a little boy. Could be my grandson. I didn't go up and talk to her, I'm not ready to do that yet."

"After I met my natural mother in Boston, I went to a shopping center to buy a present for my son. I realized that for the first time in my life I wasn't looking for a face in the crowd that looked like mine. I wasn't even aware that I had been doing that."

"I know my life won't change that much if I find out. But something is missing now. And why can't I have what everybody else has—a past?"

There were always more adoptees looking for parents than natural mothers at the meetings, and always many more women than men. I often felt that they were eyeing me, trying me on for size, asking me how I felt so that they could gauge their own mother's feelings, asking me how it happened to me in the first place. The meetings were held in the Fifth Avenue Presbyterian Church and ran all afternoon. After the meetings, I'd walk away reeling, full of emotion. We weren't crazy. The laws were.

I kept trying to get the news out, but publishers weren't interested. The story was submitted to almost every woman's magazine. The rejections were usually standard: "The material is not suitable for our magazine." Not suitable? Were they saying that the topic was unmentionable? Where did adopted children come from? Their rejections made me feel like a dirty secret that must stay swept under the rug. Once or twice there was some initial interest, and then a change of heart. Somebody said yes, somebody higher up said no. Finally, an editor from *New Woman* was interested when I mentioned the story while I was in the middle of another assignment. And at last the piece appeared. I did not use my real name, but let the editors make one up.

A friend of mine, the father of two adopted children, told me I should write under my own name; it would be better for me, for what I had to say.

"Oh, no, I can't do that—my mother doesn't know."

"Tell her. She'll understand, if she's anything like you."

"I can't. She's never going to know."

I was free-lancing as a way of life now, a precarious pursuit because there are a lot of weeks and months when you literally don't know where the rent is going to come from. And then a piece I was counting on would be rejected. Something I'd worked a month on, *the rent.* Maybe there would not be a kill fee; maybe it would be a hundred dollars, not the thousand I needed.

I would telephone my mother and tell of my desperate straits, and she would send me a few hundred dollars to tide me over. She would also ask what I was doing with my life, how come I gave up that nice job, with an office and a secretary and all.

Although I wrote articles on a variety of topics, from a profile of a balloonist to a small town's reaction to a school bus crash in which five children died to how diet affects the mind, I always found myself thinking up stories about adoption. For one magazine I wrote the story of a successful reunion between mother and daughter (and got angry when the ending was changed so it didn't appear that the adoptive mother and daughter no longer spoke). It was changed, I was told, because otherwise it made adoption seem so grim.

For *Parents,* I wrote a general piece about the issue. I interviewed the experts.

The woman seemed kindly enough. She worked for the Child Welfare League, which sets guidelines for adoption agencies around the country. Their recommendations have the force of regulations. To her, I was an innocent bystander doing a story.

"Now the records are sealed," I began. "Is that true in all states?"

"Well, a few have laws on the books in which the wording is ambiguous. That the policy to follow is the one in the best interests of all parties concerned. That is usually taken to mean that the records shall be sealed, and not opened without a court order."

"Forever sealed?"

"Uh, huh."

"Do you think that is the best policy? What do you think about adoptees coming back and asking?"

"It is very painful," she said slowly. "You should see them." She shook her head. "They come in, all nervous and timid, and have all different kinds of reasons for asking, and there are some I'd like to help. But we can't. Our hands are tied. There's nothing we can do . . . we usually recommend that they seek counseling. Some of them are *quite* disturbed."

"Couldn't their anxiety simply be because they can't find out about themselves—what you and I take for granted?"

"Well, I don't think so. They are not going to find an identity if they find out the name of their mother. And speaking of that, what do we do about the biological mother? We made a promise to them at the time that their privacy would be protected, that we would never reveal their identity."

Biological mother. Test tube. Wham bam, disappear.

"I understand, these girls are not in the best of shape when they're going through the pregnancy——"

"Oh! You should see them! They never want anybody to know, they want to keep it a secret——"

"But how do you know they stay that way?"

"Well, I guess we don't. But we feel very protective of these girls. They just want to get the arrangements over as quickly as possible, to try and forget. . . ."

"Don't you think that this is something a woman never forgets?"

"Hmmmm. I suppose so, but how can we know? We seldom hear from the mothers. They almost never come back for information, or wanting to know. It's the other way around so far, the adoptees are coming back. And more and more. Every time there's an article, we get more calls. We are thinking of reevaluating our policy. We have asked for reports from all of our member agencies as to how many are coming back, to see if this is really a trend. You know, it all fits in with different groups asking for their rights. Part of the civil rights movement."

Slaves to tradition.

"But you still will have the problem of the natural mothers. How are you going to find out what is going on in their minds? Don't you think it's likely that a lot of them might want to be found by their dau—children, and be afraid of trying to find them? Might not they feel, I gave you away once, you probably don't want to have anything to do with me?"

"I don't know how we're going to handle that one. Yes, I see what you mean, they might want to be located, but afraid of making the first move. But what about the women who gave their children away twenty, thirty years ago? Things are a lot different now, but it's possible that these women have never told their children. Or husbands, for that matter. How are they going to feel about a stranger come knocking on the door and walking in and saying, Hi, Mom?"

I pray for that day. I will handle it. I will call home and tell them I am coming home with a friend. No, I might as well tell Mother right off the bat so that she can get used to the idea. I want to meet my daughter so much it is hard to think about it because I'm afraid that it might not happen. What would I want to do? I would want to hold her and say I'm sorry it had to be this way. I'd ask are you happy and did they treat you all right and do you need anything? I'd want to tell her about her ancestors who came from Poland and the great-grandfather who was a palace guard for the czar, and how it happened that she was born and anything she would want to know. I'd take my cue from her and——

"I said, we just can't have these people walking in and wrecking lives. Don't you agree, Miss Dusky?"

"Wrecking lives . . . I see what you mean. It's a problem." Mine is a shambles because I don't know where she is. It is as simple as that. Why do I feel that there isn't a mother alive who doesn't want to know what happened, who doesn't want to meet her child? Why do I feel that every mother must feel like me? They're just afraid. Of what? What can hurt us more? I do not believe our families and friends will close us out if we speak up about yesterday's children. The more heartless it seemed then, the greater the guilt today. But when the time comes, we will purge the fury and the rage with the love of a mother for her child. No other love is so indissoluble. No matter what. No matter why.

"Is there any way you could survey these women?" I know that's not possible, not really, how are you going to track them down?

"Oh, no, dear, how could we? There's not enough staff."

They will have to speak up for themselves.

Baby, I never rejected you, please understand that. It was the idea of raising a child alone that I couldn't handle. But I love you, I have always loved you. You're my flesh and blood. I wouldn't want you to walk away from your parents. I would hope that they love you too. And be big enough to understand.

"Well, Miss Dusky, are there any further questions?"

"No, but I'd like to spend some time in your library and check some facts." Specifically to check on figures of white baby girl adoptions in 1967.

"Oh, I wasn't going to talk about this, but I might as well. I have a friend from college who was adopted. She's the most normal, intelligent person, has a lovely husband, two daughters."

I know what you are saying: She is not nuts.

"Anyway, I always knew she was adopted from the time she knew. She was going to get engaged, she was nineteen and we were in college together. When she told her mother about the engagement, her mother told her that she had something to tell her. That she was adopted. Of course, she was shocked, but they always had a pretty good relationship, so it didn't cause a rift. The mother said she had wanted to tell her earlier, but her father was always upset by it, that they couldn't have children, and he didn't want her to know that they weren't her real parents.

What are they doing with my little girl?

"Well, she went ahead and got married. Rose—her name is Rose—never said much to me about her being adopted, after she first told me. We just dropped the subject. But last year—twenty years later—we were talking on the phone and she told me that she had tried to find out what she could about her real—*biological*—mother, and she found out that she was an Irish girl who came over here and got pregnant soon after. Once the baby was born, the girl went back to Ireland. Well, one of Rose's daughters is going to Ireland this summer, and somehow Rose found out the name of her mother—I think her mother—her adoptive mother, I mean—knew the name—and the village she was from. So Rose's daughter is going to go see if she can find her. Rose told her to be careful and not to do anything to upset the woman, but if she seemed all right, to try and talk to her and tell her who she was. Isn't that the most amazing story? I would never have suspected that Rose was even curious. There's nothing lacking in her life, you know."

Is that what you really think? There is the matter of a past.

"Hmm, that story would indicate that it's not just the unhappy adoptions that make people want to know. It could be natural curiosity, don't you think?"

"I just don't know. It's so difficult. We try to do the right thing."

We all do. I couldn't think of anything else to say.

"My goodness," she said, glancing at her watch. "It's after six. I didn't realize we were talking for over an hour. I'm afraid you'll have to come back to use the library. What a nasty day. Rain all day. Well, good luck with your story. Let us know if there's anything else we can do for you. Maybe you would like to interview our director? On matters of policy, we like to have him speak. I'm sure that it can be arranged."

The rain got to me. I was in bed for a week with a cold.

I interviewed a psychoanalyst, another expert, for my article. He was a consultant to a child development agency.

"The natural parent is a stranger to the adoptee," he said. "Identity is a feeling that comes from shared experiences, sustained through years of growth, development, maturation. It does not derive from knowledge about, or the discovery of, one's biological parents. It cannot be conjured up at age forty or even at eighteen."

"What if adoptees just want to know where they came from? What if they are looking for no more than that?"

"I don't think the answer will give them the answer they are seeking. It's symptomatic of another lack in their lives. They need counseling."

"And the natural mother?"

"I feel certain that many of them do not want to be reminded of that painful time in their lives. They have made new lives for themselves. The child returning would only open the wound anew, and intensify the guilt feelings."

"Uh, huh. How do you know? Have you ever asked any of them?"

"Consider the situation. The less the woman thinks about the child the better off she is bound to be." He was dignified, gray-haired, and quite certain that he was right.

I had nothing else to ask.

I talked to a psychoanalyst from the other side. My side. He was aware of my situation.

"The mother's sense of guilt does not go away. Only when the mother can meet the grown-up child and establish in her own mind that the adoptive parents were good ones, then her guilt can be assuaged, but not before."

Yes, that's the problem, I can't find out. For instance, what if the parents were both killed in a car crash, would the family take her in? Would she find a home with an aunt or uncle? Or would the specter of *adopted* be raised? No, we don't want her, *she's not blood.* I know that sounds crazy, but it could happen. And no one would ever let me know. The child might be shunted back to the agency to look for a new adoptive home. What if they are divorced? What was it that I heard last Christmas? A couple adopted a problem child, he was six or so, and then had one of their own, and then split up, and the mother didn't want the adopted child. She only wanted her own. The husband didn't feel he could handle the child by himself. So he was sent back, the adoption undone in court. Oh my God, that can't be the case. But what if?

And what would I do if she needed and wanted to come live with me? Change my life. It is one thing to say I never wanted to have a child, but it is quite another matter once a child is born.

"How do you feel about having children yourself?" he asked.

"I don't think it will ever happen. I still feel as if it would be unfaithful to her." I shrugged. I didn't know what to make of the feeling.

"You're not alone," he said. "Sometimes the woman feels she wants to shower all her love on the one child. She feels guilty. She tells herself that she is such a bad mother she doesn't deserve another child. Other times, the woman will have other children to replace the one she gave away."

And then he said what I had been waiting to hear:

"We must assume that every adopted child is in search of the real mother. I would question someone who wasn't curious. There are few things in this world that are basically not interchangeable, and this is one of them. Every human being has a mother and a father, and it is natural to want to know who they are."

"Oh, Dr. Bach, if only that can be true . . ."

I have a friend who has an adopted daughter five years older than mine. She seems to understand exactly why I feel the way I do. She tells me that she is sure I will meet my daughter one day, but then she adds this most unusual thing: "I hope and pray Carrie doesn't try to find her biological mother. I hate the current trend of kids who are adopted getting to know their real mother. It's not because I think she would prefer her—it's just scary."

"Does Carrie ever ask about her other mother?"

"Yes. Not long ago my husband and I decided we couldn't afford to start a new magazine, which I would dearly love, and Carrie heard us talking about it. Next day she told me she had dreamed that 'that woman' came and gave her five thousand dollars so that we could start the magazine. As if five thousand dollars could do anything. But isn't that sweet?"

Yes. Sweet. But I don't understand. How would you feel about me if I were Carrie's mother?

12

Sticks and Stones

"You don't have to give your real name if you don't want to," the lawyer says on the phone. "I'm not sure I'll put you on the stand."

"Where is the courthouse? And what time?" I have just come in from dinner. I am in Washington, D.C. visiting friends. I will be in court in New York City tomorrow because I cannot turn my daughter down.

There are perhaps forty of us gathered in a huge and airless tomb of a courtroom somewhere in the Bronx. The clear February sun does not creep through the windows, which are covered with grime that looks as if it had been collecting for generations.

A forty-year-old woman named Ann Smith wants to find out who she is. That's all.

Spence-Chapin Services to Families and Children says she can't. Most of the people here today are women. Most of the people involved with this issue are women. Except the experts.

Who is more expert than I, or my daughter? Who can dare tell me that my curiosity is abnormal? Curiosity is usually considered a sign of intelligence. Not if you are adopted. Or if you have given away a child. Then it's considered neurotic. Possibly pathological. Certainly inappropriate.

What name should I use? How can I say that natural mothers want to be found if I continue to hide behind a made-up name? Is there a good reason to continue to keep this secret?

My daughter is five.

Six in a few months.

Wonder if she's in kindergarten today.

It's an open hearing. The press could be here.

From across the room, each side eyes the other. They have a few social workers; we have one, the head of an agency in Washington, D.C. She believes as we do. They have a psychiatrist. We have one coming. We also have a psychologist who has given Ann Smith a battery of tests. Lawyers. They have two; the city sent one, a black woman. And there is me: the Surprise Witness.

Am I presentable? Must look ladylike, not like a gutter person. Or a whore. That's why I wore this dress. Feminine.

You can't miss Florence, aqua sweater, flaming hair, defiant eyes, anger under the skin. Florence talks about how adoptees cannot control their own lives. Florence sometimes rants on about how this is no better than slavery. Maybe she is right: Use a separate washroom, go to the back of the bus, your records are sealed. Why?

Because. We the people have decided that it is in the best interests of the state.

Pain, and yes, a kind of hatred, steals across the room when we happen to catch each other's eyes. Each side is convinced it is absolutely right. We will win, I am sure of that. I will not go to the grave without knowing my daughter. Or I will die trying.

The other side makes a commotion about how biological mothers have gone on to make new and different lives for themselves. How pregnant and pathetic they were at the time. We agreed to keep their secret; we cannot break that code; we are honorable people.

Is that what Mrs. Hera would tell me? That she cannot break the promise she made?

I wonder what has happened to her. Used to write her for a year or two, but I haven't heard from her for ages. She left the agency. So there's no one there who knows they are keeping a promise that I never wanted.

Now they are saying *lives will be ruined . . .* that those who search have other psychological problems that are not going to clear up because they get a name of a person. Or find somebody who may not want to know them. Then the adopted child will be worse off than before.

"Excuse me, Your Honor. Will Mr. Ginns please refrain from calling them adopted *children?* We are talking about adults."

. . . and simply to satisfy idle curiosity is not worth the harm that might result. . . .

Idle curiosity?

What is this rash impulse of adopted children to find their heritage? they seem to be saying. A fad right now, part of the trend to find roots. Haven't we done right by them? Didn't we find them homes? *They were orphans.* Didn't we do our job well? How can you tell us thirty years later we have been doing the wrong thing?

The knuckles of the woman sitting next to me grow white as she grips the arm of the chair. Someone else is slinking down in her seat, aware that she is somehow being called an ingrate, even though they don't use the word. The words *biological mother* set off alarm bells in my brain.

The room is overheated and stuffy.

Our psychologist, a roly-poly figure with a fringe of white hair and a German accent, testifies that the plaintiff's Rorschach test reveals a lack of trust, isolation, constriction of affection.

Oh my God. I did that to her.

And when she draws a tree, he says, she forgets to put in the roots.

It is brought out that she once broke off an engagement with a man when she learned that he was adopted. Could be her brother. A statistical improbability? Of course. A possibility? Of course. The plaintiff is an accountant, and she would not take the chance. She is stiff and reserved in court, seemingly impassive throughout.

I'd want to hug my daughter when we meet.

And she might stand there like a stone.

Florence testifies that she spent twenty years looking for her mother and father. She found them both. She is at least at peace that she did.

I am called to the stand.

"State your name."

"Lorraine Dusky." How easy this is.

"Address."

"Three forty-three East Sixty-sixth Street. New York City."

"Occupation."

"Writer." A career lady in a flowered-print dress and black patent leather shoes. Kind to children and animals. Good with plants. A childless mother, that's it. What would the nuns say if they knew?

The people on the other side of the room are wondering what I am doing there. I have interviewed a few of them. I want to stand up and scream: Burn the courthouse! To the trenches! Drop a grenade! I am so in control that my voice is barely above a whisper.

"Would you name some of the publications your work has appeared in?"

"*Good Housekeeping, Ingenue, Cosmopolitan, Town & Country, Travel & Leisure, The New York Times.*" Yes, I sell them travel pieces occasionally.

"Do you specialize in anything?"

"I write on a number of different topics, but I have done several pieces about adoption."

"Have you interviewed many people on this subject?"

The lawyer's German accent is unmistakable. She has never given away a child, but she understands. The Nazis took her children away, after they were found hiding in a Dutch home, and when she learned they were gone, she turned herself in so she could be with them. She was sent to the camp. All of them survived. Gertrude Mainzer understands about being separated from your children.

"Yes. Fifty adoptees, at least. Maybe twenty natural mothers." The lawyer for the other side writes something down; I know that later he will try to chip away at my "expert" testimony. But I am not done yet.

"What did they say? The natural mothers."

"I never met one who didn't say that someday she

wanted to meet her child." I turn to stare down the cadre from Spence-Chapin, carefully coifed women with mouths set in ice. They shake their heads no to one another; they agree that I am some kind of nut, I speak not the truth.

"And their ages?"

"Age does not seem to make a difference, I've spoken to women who were twenty-five and women who were fifty-five. It's a hurt that does not mend with time. They all say the same thing—if only I could meet my child one day. To find out what happened. To know him or her. In this case, time does not heal all wounds."

The adversaries are now fidgeting among themselves, shrugging: Where did they get this one?

"Do you have any particular credentials for this topic?"

Here we go. "Yes. I am a natural mother myself."

Ping. Movement stops. My hands are ice cold; my brow, blazing. The judge, who has been impassive throughout, turns to me and moves closer. The head above the black robes nods, and he tells me to relax. He, at least, will not throw stones.

If only my sample were larger. If only I could say I have interviewed two hundred, two thousand, two hundred thousand of the three or four million or so natural mothers out there. I am convinced that I speak for the great majority—no, for all of them—but I have only my paltry number and gut instinct to go on. Maybe there is someone somewhere who doesn't want to be found by her child, but I find that hard to imagine. I know that you adoptive parents are afraid, but don't be. If there has been love, we cannot ruin that, nor do we want to. And I hope there is love.

The opposition chatter among themselves.

The attorney for Spence-Chapin is openly hostile.

How scientific is my research? What are my credentials that allow me to speak for other natural mothers? Am I married? Do I have other children? He is trying to make me seem like a crazy person, a voice crying out in the wilderness, an aberration of one.

"Don't you think that if the records are open it will be hard to find women who will give their children up for adoption? Knowing that they could be found one day?"

"Quite the opposite. I think knowing that you could meet your child one day would make it easier to sign the surrender papers. The absolute finality is the worst part. I didn't ask for anonymity for all time. And never from my daughter. I was told that's how it had to be."

He is annoyed. He looks up to the ceiling for a second, shakes his head. I would tell you what he looked like if I remembered.

"What about cases of abandonment?" he goes on. "Would it not be psychologically damaging for an adoptee to know he or she was abandoned?"

"The truth is better than endless fantasy. No matter what the truth is."

Who are all these people telling us what is best? They do not know. My voice rises, yet I feel as if I am sitting back and watching this drama unfold.

"Don't you believe there are other natural mothers— the ones who do not come forward—who would rather forget what happened, forget that part of their lives?"

"You don't have someone in your body for nine months and forget."

Robert Jay Lifton, author of ten books, psychiatrist, Yale professor, our expert ace in the hole, is called to the stand in the afternoon. Our attorney begins the questioning.

"Could you explain to us how the identity of an adult or an adolescent is shaped, in your opinion?"

Dr. Lifton does not hesitate; his voice is clear, assured. "The identity of an adolescent—or any of us—is shaped from at least two general directions. From the sense of his or her ongoing relationship with his or her parents, whether they are natural or adoptive parents; and on the basis of social and historical factors.

"Identity isn't any one thing. It is a configuration, and it depends very much upon one's sense of relationship over the generations to one's heritage; one's biological and historical roots as well as one's immediate life history in relation to one's immediate parents. The one is insufficient without the other."

"Is it your professional opinion that the need for historical connectiveness is important for any adolescent or adult, or only for those with specific problems or conflicts?"

"No. One's sense of relationship to one's own history is very important to all of us. It is by no means limited in any way to somebody in conflict or somebody particularly disturbed, nor is it limited to the adopted person. It is general."

"What is the special situation of an adult who has been adopted?"

"An adopted person not only has all the human struggles that everyone has, but also has undergone a dislocation. This means that identity for the adoptive person is not a single issue, but includes both the immediate relationship with the psychological parents and the historical and biological connections with one's sense of heritage. Both needs become very intense because of that dislocation."

Dislocated. It is as if I sent her up in a balloon, without a tether to the ground, and wherever she lands, *she lands.* Where did you come from, dear? Oh, I see the balloon brought you. Well, let's forget about where that came from.

"This dislocation is not necessarily a source of pathology, but it can be a source of great disturbance."

"Would you not consider it sufficient for the adult adoptee to identify with the historical background of his adoptive family?"

"It is the most natural and desirable aspect of any adolescent or young adult to have curiosity about his forebears, about his biological heritage and the sequence of his generational connectedness. Incidentally, that curiosity is immediately stimulated by the very announcement that he or she is adopted. It is inevitable.

"And the more lies and false stories about how his or her parents died in an automobile crash, which is a common myth, the more the relationship between the adopted person and adopted parents is clouded by dishonesty and illusion.

"The curiosity will occur in fantasies and in distorted ways that we encourage now by keeping this a dark secret, or it will occur quite naturally with answers of honesty as the subject is brought up. But it will occur in any case."

In any case.

"Do you believe that continued secrecy at this point might contribute to the security of the growing up child or might it lead to other consequences?"

"I think that continued secrecy about the information concerning one's natural parents poisons the relationship between the adoptive parents and the adopted person. What it does is build an aura of guilt and conflict over that very natural, very healthy, very inevitable curiosity. Secrecy always breeds guilt.

"The origin of the secrecy is the specter of illegitimacy in the background. Instead of confronting these issues openly, there is the pretense that they don't exist and the whole subject becomes pervaded with guilt in a way that harms that relationship between the adopted child and his or her psychological parents. Every adopted person I have spoken to has confirmed that process."

"Does this need for complete information on the part of the adult adoptee or adolescent include knowledge of his original name?"

"Very much so. A name is an enormously important element of identity over the generations and over the course of one's individual life. Moreover, by learning the name, by learning about the person—one's mother and father—he or she becomes an actual vibrant human being rather than fragmented bits of information. Such bits and pieces, ethnic or social characteristics, medical background, only become further stimulants to curiosity.

"From my own experience with adopted people and from the literature, it apparently seems as though every single adopted person has some significant curiosity about this.

"Some are blocked from further effort by that layer of guilt; others make no effort. But the desire to find out is probably universal. Where it is blocked, one remains locked in more extreme fantasies. The fantasies that adopted children seem to have are at either extreme: The mother is either imagined to be a prostitute in the gutter of society— otherwise, why would they keep this dirty little secret—or, at the other extreme, a great queen that will lift one out of one's ordinary existence into something noble.

"Neither extreme is healthy or real. I think that one is locked into conflict and there is enormous frustration in not being able to find one's identity. I would sum this up by saying a gap in one's sense of identity will always remain if one cannot find out this information about one's heritage.

"I don't want to give the impression that these things run perfectly smoothly and harmoniously. Even after the adopted person finds out who his or her real mother and father are, there are bound to be conflicts because the nature of the relationship is unclear.

"However, there is some profound satisfaction that is achieved. One's sense of identity comes closer to reality."

Yes. I understand, the nature of our relationship is unclear. And will always be. But I am dying to know you. I ache inside whenever I think of you. So many things to remind me. And now they are telling me how hard it will be for you to figure out who you are. I know I can never change the way things are. Your life is already irrevocably stamped because you are adopted.

You could reject me if you wanted to. You could say, just give me the information, that is all that I need, you didn't want me before and I don't want you now, and I would take it. You have that right. Oh, I wouldn't like it, I would give anything to love you. I love you now, but my love goes up in the air and floats around, looking for a home, looking at faces in a crowd. Why can't you have all the love you can get?

I wish someone would open a window. I can't breathe.

The cross-examination begins. The opposition speaks.

"If a person did not have this specific link—of being connected from one generation to another—what sort of conditions might this person exhibit?"

Yes. Just what have I done to my daughter?

"You cannot maintain a mono-causal view: There is no psychological condition that is caused by any one thing," Dr. Lifton says. "If the adopted person becomes neurotic, it does not depend solely on being adopted, or conflict with the mother or father. It is the combination.

"But what I can't seem to emphasize enough is that this gap in identity contributes to a sense of distance from other people, a sense of unreality, that adopted people consistently feel. You see, they have no organic link that they know of, and the psychological relationship to that link is very important."

He means she is very lonely, no matter what.

She wants to know where she comes from. I want to know where she went.

"Then it is your opinion that if the adoptee never were to find his or her biological parents, he could never lead a normal life?"

"I didn't say that. I said if the adoptee never finds his or her parents, he or she goes through life with a gap in identity, a sense of distance or lack of intimacy in most relationships.

"But we have people going through life in what seem to be normal ways with all sorts of conflicts and difficulties. If there are added elements, that particular stress could help push one over into some sort of suffering, conflict, neurosis, or whatever."

I was led to believe she would be better off without me. This is much worse than I have ever imagined.

". . . I am not questioning the principle of confidentiality. But it becomes absurd when it no longer serves its original purpose. In my experience with a few natural mothers in the course of my work, they seem to have, quite understandably, a deep ambivalence. In a number of cases there is enormous relief over having found the natural child, now an adult, or being found by the adult adoptee—enormous relief from a gnawing feeling of guilt and anxiety that had never left them. You know, they don't wipe out their history by decree. They live with it.

"But there is enormous relief that the child they left with another family has now found some degree of happiness or has been able to get through life with some degree of achievement."

Oh, my baby, of course I would want you to be strong, beautiful, accomplished, with gifts that are worthy of song, but I shall love you no matter what. You are my daughter.

There is an old Arab proverb: A monkey is a gazelle in the eyes of his mother.

"We have heard today testimony to the effect that a child's knowledge that he would be able to obtain this complete information when he reached his majority would weaken his bonds with his adoptive parents and would also be against the best interests of the adoptee. Do you agree with that statement?"

"I disagree on both counts," Dr. Lifton continues. "I think in all fairness to the adoptive parents, it is very hard for them now to come to this new idea of the adopted person's having access to his or her records. It is quite threatening.

"But the reason it is threatening is that we have built the whole subject around the illusion that one can black out this aspect of history, or the heritage of the adopted person.

"I think in the long run as we adopt this policy, of integrity and fidelity, of being more open, not only will the identity of the adopted person take firmer root in ways I have begun to suggest, but the relationship between the adopted children and the adoptive parents will be improved from the beginning because it will be a relationship built around honesty, rather than deception."

The truth shall set ye free.
So it will.
I am going to go home and tell Mother.
She'll survive.
Florence reaches over and touches my arm. My eyes are filling with tears.

13

Setting the Record Straight

A few weeks after the day in court, I went home to Michigan. I took my mother to lunch at a fancy restaurant where I knew we could sit side by side on a banquette. I wanted to be able to touch her.

We ordered gin and tonics and broiled scrod.

"Mother, remember that time I told you I had mono?" I could see the quizzical look on her face, but I kept right on going. "I didn't have mono, I had a baby then."

The words rifled across her face. And then her hand was on mine. "How was your labor?"

"It was all right."

"What did you have?"

"A girl."

"Oh, honey . . ."

We quietly cried then, we didn't make a scene, we sent the fish back untouched with apologies. I told her about Brian, how I didn't feel I had a choice, how I felt I couldn't come home.

"Honey, your father and I talked about what we would do if this ever happened. We decided that we would keep the baby and raise it as our own."

I have to tell myself that it was not meant to be.

Then my mother talked about her father. How they never got along, how she felt he always treated her differently from her sisters. My mother and I had been through some rough times, but now all the reasons seemed silly. In the space of this moment, a bridge we had never been able to find before was crossed.

Although I had turned out differently from what she'd planned, I was her daughter; that was enough. And now she understood that I had completed the rite of passage into womanhood; I had a child. I understood what grown-up ladies understood. I was a woman in full standing. From now on everything would be different between us. We would be mother and daughter, but equals.

I told my mother that day about the movement of adoptees to open up their sealed birth records, and how I had become involved over the years. I told her that from now on, I was going to use my real name.

"You have got to get used to the idea that one day you might turn on the TV and see me talking about this. The articles I write will appear under my by-line." She nodded. Understand, my mother is no crusader, or at least I hadn't thought so.

"There are a lot of people who think we are wrong, who are trying very hard to keep those records sealed. But I am not going to stop this until it's over. Until the records are open. Until my daughter is free to find us.

Maybe by the time she is eighteen, the records will be open."

She was silent for no longer than a heartbeat. "I think you are doing the right thing. Of course you have to use your real name. It doesn't make any sense otherwise." She paused again, sighed.

"I think if I were adopted," she said, "I think I would want to know who my real parents were. Just to know. They must all want to know, no matter how good their adopted parents are to them. Wouldn't you want to know?"

She didn't really need an answer from me. We both had tears in our eyes again.

"Honey, we've got to hope that she has good parents. That they're taking good care of her. They're her parents too." Yes, Mama, I know.

And then she added: "Oh, honey, I only hope I live long enough to meet her."

Several months passed. The court ruled that while Ann Smith could examine her city records—which contained no identifying information—she was denied access to her file at Spence-Chapin Services to Families and Children. The judge noted in his decision that her agency file did not contain information that would reveal the identity of her biological parents.

But he still ruled that she could not see it, because somehow that was not in her best interests, because that would have been setting legal precedents, because that would have opened a can of worms.

I wrote a piece about the trial for the *Times* Op-Ed page; I revealed that I was a natural mother and a former member of the board of directors of ALMA. The editor of the page was my old boss; she had been promoted. She asked me to cut the story, held it for almost a year, and then ran it with a huge sketch to illustrate it. The drawing shows a child in a buggy reaching for a figure of a woman shadowed in black. There are several trees in the picture; the leaves seem to be weeping. I was in the Yucatán when it ran.

A few years later, in Albany testifying at a hearing about the records, I get the usual response when I appear to talk about my daughter. The chatter and rustlings cease, I feel everybody looking at me, the one who is supposed to be ashamed and embarrassed. People are amazed that I would talk about it publicly.

I have my moment, and then I am attacked. "If there exists one natural mother who doesn't want to know her child, does that mother have a right to anonymity?"

You are talking about an infinitesimally small number, I insist.

"But what if she exists—that one person who wants her privacy—does she have a right to it? How can we open the records without hurting this woman?"

Silence.

"She has no right to privacy from her child. You have a baby, you have a responsibility to that person, no matter what. And remember this: When I signed that paper, for whatever reasons, I had the option of making a choice. An adopted person does not. He was never asked what is in his best interests."

An old man sitting in front of me sighed—loud, exasperated, disgusted. I later learned he was Shad Polier, legal counsel to an adoption agency in Manhattan, and a civil rights lawyer whose involvement goes back to the Scottsboro Boys case forty-five years earlier. And more than a decade ago, he drafted the first state law on termination of parent's rights when the children are held in foster care too long.

He got his chance to disagree with me when he was on the stand.

Why is he so protective of the natural mothers he has never met? I think that he must hear stories about the poor pregnant girls who want the secret in their belly hidden. From anyone. But does he know these women two decades later? Like so many others peripherally involved, he had such strong opinions. But like divorce and giving birth and losing a loved parent, this is one one of those things you can't quite understand until it happens to you.

A few months after the hearing, I read about Shad Polier on the obituary page of *The New York Times*. I was riding a bus and saw his picture. The words told me that he was a man with convictions not unlike some of my own, yet somehow he came to believe that my daughter's right to know was not as critical as my right to privacy. How did he get it so wrong?

Shad Polier was seventy; he would not have changed his mind. I cannot help but think: And now the opposition is dying.

The Kickerbocker News put my picture on the front page. I talked to my old boss that evening. He never knew about my child until that day.

A few weeks after the hearing, I was having a business lunch with a public relations executive. I was now a senior editor at *Town & Country*. The lunch had been postponed when I went to Albany to testify; I say I was in Albany, and he asks why. I consider simply saying "business." With strangers, with men especially, I am so often silent because the topic can easily become a moment's embarrassment or an hour's conversation. There are times when I am just weary. But for some reason, I tell the whole truth today.

"I hope you don't mind hearing this, but I have an adopted daughter," he says. I've been through this before, but I can't help asking right off the bat: "How old is she?"

"Twenty."

One down.

"I don't want to hurt you," he continues, barely noticing my question, "but something happened last year that I think might interest you."

I nod for him to continue.

"Last year we got a call from the adoption agency where we found our daughter. She's a lovely girl, she's in college, we think the world of her."

Relax. I am sure you are terrific parents. And why do you have to assure me that she's a lovely girl? Are you telling me she doesn't have bad blood?

"Anyway, the agency called and said that her parents wanted to meet her. They were in college when our daughter was born. They got married later and moved to California, and the man has become quite successful in business. And they have three children. Well, the couple came to New York on a visit and went to the agency because they wanted to meet our daughter. Now I know you aren't going to like this, but we said no."

"Your daughter didn't want to meet them?"

"We didn't ask her. She's never once expressed interest in meeting her natural parents, and if she had just once said she wanted to meet them . . ."

I wonder if I have ever met his daughter at an ALMA meeting. I wonder if he's the father of one of the guilty ones, someone who can't speak the truth to her parents, and so lies with her silence.

I want to throw my drink at him and storm out of the Oak Room at the Plaza Hotel, like Bette Davis must have done in some movie.

"What gives you the right to speak for her?" is what comes out of my mouth.

He shrugs. We change the topic of conversation. I am there to do business, after all, not to throw a tantrum.

Pray God, don't let her parents be like him.

We say good-bye on the corner of Fifty-sixth Street and Fifth Avenue. Cars, people, noise, everybody going somewhere.

14

A Photograph in a Magazine

What's so special about this photograph? Why is Barbara standing here with a big grin on her face, waiting for me to say something? Two famous writers and their daughter in Topanga Canyon. What is this? *People* magazine. I know Barbara loves to collect stories about how writers write, but so—that girl looks like my cousins. As they used to look at the family picnics when I was a kid. She looks like I did. Sort of.

"She's adopted," Barbara finally blurts out, "and she's ten!"

Oh my God. Stringy blonde hair. Like mine. Big for her age. So were Brian's other kids, he told me. Round face—she could be Polish. The shape of my face. The eyes—not really. But her nose—not turned up that one—looks like mine did at the age, before it popped out big. I always wondered if this would happen and now it has and can this really be true? And Barbara found her. I wouldn't have the nerve to think it. Barbara and I were roommates at the time.

"Does it say so in the story?"

"Right here—look. I was reading it last night, and I didn't think anything at first when I read the part about her being adopted, and ten, but then I looked at the pictures again. There are more on the next page. She even looks more like you in this one of her washing the car with Paley. I couldn't wait until you got home. I almost called you out at Judy's, but then I figured you wouldn't be able to get the magazine last night and would go out of your mind." I'd been staying with friends out in Sag Harbor, a summer resort town on Long Island. It was August.

The chances of this actually happening are minuscule. Stay calm. But wait a minute—in the picture washing the car, she looks like she's got long arms. Like me.

Like her mother.

I'm flushed and my temples are beating and I can feel the heavy pounding of my heart. I have to make sure. I have to find out so that there is no doubt. *I can't believe I am even thinking this.* Barbara understands. Her own cousin gave away a child and then tried to kill herself. Calm now. Do not become a crazy lady.

"Barbara, I have to find out for sure. But this is my daughter. I know it. I feel it."

"Certainly looks like she could be. Her eyes look more like Brian's."

Barbara had met Brian quite by accident. Both writers, they were covering the same story, standing next to one another at a press conference.

"Her name is stranger than fiction—Palenque," Barbara says. "What exactly is that?"

Of course. It would be Palenque. I was in the land

of the Maya a few years ago, hitchhiking and riding buses.

I flew to the heart of the Yucatán, where a wild scrub jungle is home to a primitive and proud people, where the Maya ruled in dignity, where virgins were sacrificed to appease the gods, where temples were built that contain the secrets of the stars, where the wind whips through the bush and singes the soul. Tulum, ancient city, a temple that stands high above the ocean, so indelibly turquoise. I sat near the top of the temple on a ledge put into place centuries ago; there were swimmers below. I was just a wanderer passing through.

I didn't go to Palenque, I nearly did but then at the last minute changed my mind, and so I missed Palenque, and so of course that would be her name.

I read and reread the article. I learn that Palenque may have held their marriage together. Don't like the sound of that. They may change residences so that Palenque can go to school elsewhere. That means they care. It says they have money. That means they can give her horseback riding lessons and ballet classes and well, everything.

Except what I could.

Books, lots of them, I'll bet. And music and poetry. The father looks wonderful. Kind. Funny. But the mother —doesn't she look a little pinched, too thin, is she spare with her love? No. Possessive, maybe. She is staring so hard at her daughter. Be glad for what you get. If you could have, you would have chosen them. Professional people, that's what Mrs. Hera said. Who would have thought it would be the same profession?

I pull out my childhood pictures. Yes, Barbara agrees, they look like Palenque. Remarkable, she says. Especially one of me in a gypsy costume, ready for Halloween.

It is close to midnight on this summer Sunday night.

From the article I learn that he is Irish-Catholic, like Brian.
A match, like the agencies say they try to do.

I know she's the one. God wouldn't trick me like this.
Good night, Palenque. Palenque Paley. How many letters are there? Thirteen! Thirteen letters! Of course it is
A Sign. I was born on the thirteenth, my parents met on
the thirteenth, they married on the thirteenth, and I was
baptized on the thirteenth. I have found my daughter.
Thank you, Barbara and *People* and God, if you are there.

Sleep is different that night.

I do not keep this secret. ALMA's attorney is struck
by the resemblance. Florence is convinced. She shows
the magazine to her husband, who has met me twice, and
says, "Whose daughter do you think she is?"

"Jesus Christ—Lorraine's!" is the way the story comes
back to me.

A search is undertaken for articles, interviews, and
biographies of the two people who are the parents. Barbara
finds an old clipping from a Florida newspaper. Palenque
is quoted as saying that she wants to be an actress. I
had just finished a draft of a novel in which an adopted
teen-ager wants to be an actress. My heroine is talented,
naturally, but part of the reason she wants to be an actress
is that when she is interviewed she can say she was adopted
and ask that her birthdate be in the story.

I learn who among my acquaintances have interviewed
them.

The mother was actually in *Town & Country* a few
years before I joined the staff. "Steve, when you were out
there did you see the daughter, Palenque?"

"Yeah. She wasn't there the whole time, but she came
in during the interview. Nice looking kid. Big for her
age."

"I know this might seem absurd—but you didn't happen to ask when her birthday was?"

"Whose?"

"Palenque's."

"No. That's a rather strange question, don't you think? Why do you ask?"

"Uh . . . I think she's my daughter. She's adopted, you know? The age is right, she looks like me—Barbara found her picture and thought so right away. And from what I've figured out, the adoptive parents were living in New York and moved to California that year. She could be from New York. Lots of people move to a different state after they adopt. And anyway, lots of writers live in Topanga Canyon."

"Are you kiddin? *Holy Christ.*"

"I have got to find out for sure." I'd better change the subject now. He thinks I'm off my rocker. "Listen, I heard your piece on South Africa is great. We're changing the magazine so we can run all of it. What did it run to? Seventy pages?"

I show the photograph to Linda, *Town & Country*'s art director.

"She's adopted—she's my daughter's age."

"Lorraine, I just got goose pimples. She looks so much like your daughter. What do you think?"

"What do I think? I think she's my daughter."

"What are you going to do?"

"Find out. For sure. I have to find out for sure."

"What will you do then?"

"I don't know. Maybe I could talk to them."

An interview with the mother appears in *Ms.* It says Palenque's birth certificate is kept in a safe-deposit box.

Why? Do they have the original one? The one with the original name, my name?

The father writes a magazine piece about Palenque. She has made a doll house on several shelves of her bookcase. One room is the projection room. So that is how she lives. She still wants to be an actress.

She is communicating with me. Why not this way?

I put her picture on my bulletin board, next to one of me as a child. I know my friends are dubious. They see the photograph, and they get this doubtful and concerned look on their faces. I do not care. I know I will prove that I am right.

My latest article on the topic of adoption is brought to the attention of the producers of the *Today* show. They ask me to be interviewed with Rod McKuen and a man from Michigan, an adoptee who has found his mother, and who may or may not be in favor of opening the records. It is hard to tell where he stands, except that like so many adoptees I have known, he seems to want everyone's approval. To make up for that first rejection.

McKuen's book *Finding My Father* has just come out, and he talks about the pain of not knowing, and how the questions were at least answered when he tracked down his father and found him dead.

When asked if I am sorry I gave my daughter away, I say I am sorry that I had to give her to people I don't know.

"Do you have any idea where she might be?"

"No." Are you folks watching out there? Look at my face. Look at your daughter's face.

The interviewer refers to me as someone who is searching for her daughter. I do not like the sound of that because it sounds as if I want to take her back. No,

I do not want to ruin her life, but yes, I would change mine if necessary, if she needed that, if she needed me.

But I can't find out anything.

A few years ago I wrote to the agency and asked *How is she doing? Can't I know? Maybe she needs me.* The reply said she was adopted by people who were curious about me. They will convey to her that you loved her. How? Unless I say them, the words are meaningless, a smoke screen for everybody to hide contentedly behind.

I walk off the set, and a well-dressed young woman who must have something to do with the show grabs my arm. We are standing in the deep shadows of a curtain. "It's hard," she begins quietly, "isn't it?"

I nod.

"I have a twelve-year-old son. I wonder if he'll ever want to find me. You never forget, do you? I'm married now—I even have another child—but I never stop wondering what happened to him." She pauses, but she is not waiting for me to say anything. I recognize in her voice the same shaky ground of guilt and sorrow on which we live. "My husband knows. I'll tell my daughter when she is older."

"Do you think those records will ever be open?"

"They have to be."

"I can't do what you are doing. Be so public, I mean. But don't give up."

I clasp her hand and nod. Our eyes meet. There's not really anything more that needs to be said.

In the drizzly rain, I walk from the NBC studio in Rockefeller Center back to work. I have on a gray flannel suit and a navy silk shirt. I look like the career woman I always wanted to be.

When I get to the office, I find that almost everyone was there early to watch me on a set in someone's office.

Linda has given me six red roses, and the editor has decided to send me to Morocco. There are a few phone
messages from adopted people I know.

I have dinner with an old friend, an editor who knows
the adoptive parents. He hears me out. He says, "You must
find out, one way or the other."
He says he will help. Just ask. Not yet, I say.

A month later, a friend of a friend of theirs comes
up with the information that the daughter is from New
York State. And that same afternoon, someone tells me she
believes the daughter was born in April.

Fifty letters or more come my way as a result of the
Today show. Some are from adoptees telling me I gave
them the courage to admit to their adoptive families they
want to search, some tell me of searches with happy end-
ings, some are long, handwritten pages that should go to
a psychiatrist rather than me. Some are from other natural
mothers who feel as I do. Some are from adoptive parents
who tell me I should adopt a child or do volunteer work
with children. Some say they pray for me, some say I am
sick. One of the writers says she knows an adopted girl
who looks so much like me she must be my daughter. When
I answer with the pertinent information, I receive no reply.
An article about me and the movement appears in a
New Jersey newspaper. There is a photograph of me in my
office. There is a wistful look on my face. I am staring
off into space.

It is a Saturday morning two weeks later. The phone
rings. I hear the background clicks that usually signify
long distance.

"Is this Lorraine Dusky?"

"Yes. Who is this?"

"I can't tell you. But I haven't been able to sleep since I saw your picture in the paper. My daughter looks so much like you—the eyes, the mouth, the color of hair. Only your cheeks are fuller. Even my husband—he's a conservative type—sees the resemblance. I keep thinking the neighbors did too. The article said your daughter was ten. Did you mean that literally? Did you mean *about* ten?"

Who is this and is this the mother of my child?

Bambambam, adrenaline rush. "How old is your daughter?" We are playing with one another, to see who will first reveal the missing information.

"She's eleven."

Not mine. "My daughter is ten."

But the caller wants to know the exact birthdate, since she is not yet convinced because I look so much like her daughter who has a million friends, her daughter who is gifted in every way possible, more than any daughter she and her husband could ever have had.

The day and the month do not match either. The stranger on the other end of the connection sighs. I am not sure whether the mismatch brings relief or not. She says she was going to hang up if the information corresponded, without telling me who she is. She says she knows that it would break her daughter's heart if one day she had to give a child away. Why does she think her daughter will be faced with that choice? Like mother, like daughter? The only thing I am sure of is that I don't know what I feel, that the emotions are tumbling out, waiting to be told which gear to shift into.

She won't tell me where she is calling from.

She says she knows I must love my daughter, and she is sure that someday we'll find one another. And what do you want your daughter to do? Then we go over some of the same conversation because—for some reason—we are looking for a reason to continue the connection, pointless though it seems. Each of us recognizes that while we wish the other party were the missing person, we are also afraid of that reality.

But Palenque is my daughter, I keep repeating.

She and I go on for another minute or two in this limbo, and I realize that just as I fantasize about two other people, she has been fantasizing about me. I seem as though I would make a good mother for her child. How odd that sounds to my ears. We hang up and I spend the rest of the day—or maybe week—trying to get over the phone call from everyone, from no one in particular.

Am I as absurd about those people in California as this woman is about me? No. I have found my daughter. Say it enough and it will be true.

I phone Brian a few days later and tell him about the conversation, and about Palenque. We seldom speak, but we do keep in touch. Our daughter is a link that refuses to break. He listens patiently and says that one day he too wants to meet this other child of his, but I can sense the caution in his voice. He thinks I am a little crazy. I am not. But I do not wish to speak to him long this day.

I acquire their address. I put it in my appointment book.

Her birthday comes, and I mull over sending a card. I

decide against it. A new friend brings me a bunch of daffodils and takes me to dinner. We toast her birthday. It is, all things considered, a pleasant evening.

Her mother has a new book out. More interviews, more mention of Palenque. And in *Time* magazine, Palenque turns eleven at just the right time. I am positive. I only need the final piece of information to be sure. I am, however, afraid to write them. They will be worried about me. Someone calls *Time* for me to see if the researcher has the exact date. She does not. She is indignant—why not call them yourself? Why not, indeed?

The only person who dares to say that no matter how much circumstantial data I am collecting, she feels that I am mistaken is an old friend. One day I learned she had also given a child away. We did not know that when we became friends.

When I told her about me, we were having lunch, having a nice time.

"Oh my God," she said and knocked over a glass of water. "Me too."

So now when she tells me that she thinks I am wrong, this cannot be, I do not object or take umbrage, for after all, surely she understands this madness. She says I must find out for sure.

The pieces begin not to fit. The girl is from California, not New York as I had thought. They saw her on the first day of her life. Can't be. They got her through a private physician. Also wrong.

My world begins to crumble, my assurance is dissolving, but I will not believe Palenque is not my daughter until I hear it from them.

I try to work. I cannot. Read. My mind wanders. Go to the gym. Don't feel like it. I try to phone the friend who never believed Palenque was mine, but I can't remember her number this day. I leave a message on her machine. I continue to stare into space or at the picture of Palenque on my bulletin board over my desk. My friend calls. She tells me to call the adoptive parents. I obey. I get their number. I dial. A secretary answers. I leave my name and number. They do not call back. They do not know who I am, a stranger calling with a New York City number. I feel nothing. I told everyone I could handle this.

"Well, Lorraine, I guess you don't have to write them." It is Barbara speaking.

"Write them? Of course I have to. The facts could be wrong. They could have their reasons for obscuring the truth."

"But so many? The information is very specific. I don't think they would make up so much."

"I have to be sure. I will believe it when he tells me. Not before."

"I know I'm the one who started all this when I noticed the resemblance, but it's over now. I was talking to Ellen at work and she agrees too. You have to face facts. You don't need to write them."

Wonderful. Now my craziness is reduced to office gossip.

"Look, I am going to write them. OK? I don't want to talk about this anymore." She doesn't have a child, she doesn't understand.

"Lorraine, I didn't realize how upset you were about this, how deep this is. I'm sorry."

"It's OK."

Good night, my baby, wherever you are, whoever you are. Good night Palenque with the thirteen letters in your name.

Almost a month passes. If anyone asks me if I've written, I say "not yet." And then on a Saturday afternoon, when I've got too many errands to run, I dash off a note, without poetics or emotion. I state my facts—or rather, the real ones, the ones that relate to the birth of my daughter—and ask for particulars. Her picture is on my wall. She is mine until he tells me she is not.

The letter is not mailed until Monday.

On the following Monday, June 13, I receive several pieces of mail. There are a few birthday cards. And there is a letter from him. There is no address on the envelope, but the handwriting is strange to me and the postmark is *California*. I bring it up to my room. I sit down at my desk. I use a letter opener, an antique my father gave me.

Her picture comes down. It is filed somewhere.

15

A Message for My Daughter

Hello, baby, I am writing this to you. It is strange and wonderful to think you might read it. It is like putting a letter in a bottle and flinging it into the sea.

You will be thirteen. It seems like just yesterday you were struggling for your life in an incubator, and now you are almost grown up. Your body is changing, and your breasts may be starting. What are girls your age like? Long straight hair, blue jeans, peasant blouses and espadrilles. Giggles on the bus from school. The first telephone calls from boys. Girl friends who share all your secrets. Or maybe you're not like that at all. I wasn't. Not really.

Are you alive? Are you?

There's so much to say I am having a hard time beginning.

I write to the agency where you were adopted every now and then. Somebody writes back, the person is always changing, and they have told me that they put the letters in our file and that if you ever come back and ask, they will give them to you. I sent a picture too. I don't look like that anymore. Something about me has changed. I'll send another one soon.

The first letter that I got back from the agency said you were adopted by a couple who "have been most delighted" with you. And what about you? Are you delighted too? The letter also said that during the home study the parents talked extensively about their feelings toward the natural parents. "They will surely convey the idea that the child was surrendered because her mother loved her." That's not really right. Of course, I love you, but I didn't give you away because I loved you; I gave you away because I couldn't keep you. I try to tell myself that it was meant to be this way, that you came out of me and him and that you were supposed to grow up with those people, whoever they are, and there are times when I can accept that quite calmly.

Not very often.

Your grandmother is still alive, and we talk about you frequently. In a way, you're part of our family too, right now. She said she was going to change her will and leave you, in a trust, the same amount of money she is leaving her three other grandchildren. It's not much, but we want you to know that we think of you. And one time, she told me that when she dies, she wants on her gravestone *four grandchildren,* no matter who knows and who doesn't and who asks questions.

But we don't think she is going to die until she meets you. She tells her friends that she is going to live some years yet, and when they ask her how she knows, she simply says: "I've got something to live for," and then she smiles and that's that.

She has a plant at home for you too. It's a baby's

tears that someone gave her, and when she's watering it or moving it around so that it gets enough sunshine, she thinks about me and she thinks about you. It's growing like mad.

People often say to me that they know I'll meet you one day. But what if you don't want to know me? What if you aren't even curious? What if you are so angry you won't look me up, even if you can? But when somebody says, I know she will, I get all shaky inside and I wait a few minutes until it passes. I collect all these things in my heart, and if I think on them hard enough, maybe it will happen. Sometimes I stop in the Catholic church near here and just sit and wonder about you and light a candle too.

I don't mean to sound pathetic. I've made a good life for myself. Time passes and the phone rings and the sun comes up. I laugh and dance and have people over. The man in my life understands about you and how I feel. Maybe one day you will meet him.

I have something bad to tell you. You know those birth control pills I took when I didn't think I was pregnant? The doctor gave them to me. Well, it turns out they can hurt you. I read it in a medical journal. It might not mean anything, but you should be examined regularly to make sure there is no abnormality. You should start being examined by the time you are fourteen. It is very important.

The statistics aren't as frightening as if I had taken another hormone some pregnant women took—DES—but there still is a chance that the pills could have affected you; you have got to be cautious. I found out about it this last summer when I was researching an article.

I wrote and told the lady at the agency—I wrote three

times, in fact, before I got an answer—and she said someone would get in touch with your parents and let them
know. But I worry that your parents won't believe me,
that they may think it's just a trick to communicate with
you. I have asked the agency to let me know when they
have contacted your parents. It's only been a month.

I hope your parents don't think I am some kind
of pariah come back to haunt them, or hurt them. I hope
they understand I don't want to hurt you. That's the last
thing I'd ever want. I don't imagine that if I found you,
your life with them would change that much; you just
can't walk out on what I hope has been a lifetime of love.
But I could tell you what happened. I could ask you to
forgive me.

Yes, I'd like to have you visit me. You could call me
Lorraine, it would be fine. I'd just like to see you. Even
if I couldn't talk to you.

You have two uncles and three first cousins, and a
whole bunch of other relatives who already know about
you. I sometimes imagine flying home to Detroit with you
to meet my mother. She'd be at the airport, make no
mistake. She always picks me up when I come home for
Christmas.

We always talk about you on Christmas, my mother
and me. Sometimes she calls me around your birthday, if
not on the exact date, and I know she says a lot of prayers
for you. And there are forsythia in the living room that I
am forcing into bloom. You will be thirteen tomorrow.

Some people may question why I wrote this book. I
had to get in touch with you. It seemed the best way.

And I am tired of hearing about how natural mothers

don't want to be found. I so desperately want to know you one day. I want those laws changed.

I'm going to sign off now, but remember that we're all hoping and praying and waiting for you.

All my love,

Lorraine